STUDY GUIDE FOR OREGON

REAL ESTATE

AGENCY

JOHN JEDDELOH

Published in the United States of America by
Real Estate Publishers, Inc.
8316 N. Lombard #329
Portland, Oregon 97203-3727

WWW.REALESTATEPUBLISHERS.COM
E-mail: INFO@REALESTATEPUBLISHERS.COM

Library of Congress Catalog Card Number 99-66090
ISBN 1-878572-18-0

First printing, September 2002
Second printing, January, 2004
(With revised seller's property disclosure)

Cover Design: Architectural elevation of house © 2002 Bruinier & Associates, Inc., Portland, Oregon, 800-379-3828, reproduced with permission. Bruinier & Associates sells stock building plans and plan books for residential, commercial, duplexes, rowhouses and multifamily. Plans are available in traditional format or on CD-ROM. They also do custom architectural design. You can see their work at HTTP://WWW.BRUINIER.COM, or e-mail PLANS@BRUINIER.COM.

Contents

Introduction

The *STUDY GUIDE FOR OREGON REAL ESTATE AGENCY* offers a thorough introduction to real estate agency relationships in Oregon and is especially structured to prepare students to take the Oregon real estate license examinations. The text is part of the Study Guide series – other texts in the series include *STUDY GUIDE FOR OREGON REAL ESTATE LAW*, *STUDY GUIDE FOR OREGON REAL ESTATE FINANCE*, *STUDY GUIDE FOR OREGON REAL ESTATE PRACTICES*, *STUDY GUIDE FOR OREGON REAL ESTATE CONTRACTS* and *STUDY GUIDE FOR OREGON PROPERTY MANAGEMENT*. Used in conjunction with the other texts in the series, this text will give the reader an excellent foundation in real estate. It is an invaluable tool for anyone interested in real estate investments, property management, mortgage lending, title work, escrow and real estate development.

This book is divided into several sections covering all aspects of the practical side of real estate agency issues, with special consideration to those topics which are covered on Oregon real estate licensing examinations. Because many people using this book will be preparing for the examinations, we have taken great care to ensure that all examination subjects are covered thoroughly, and in proportion to their importance on the real estate examinations. In addition, we have included sample examination questions, many of which have been used on past state exams.

The author, John Jeddeloh, began his real estate career in 1971 and since then has worked in sales, brokerage, property management, appraisal, investments, and as an educator.

The sample questions and text material are from the author's personal knowledge of the real estate licensing examinations in Oregon, from his many years of teaching prelicense courses in both public and private schools in Oregon. The author has 20 years of classroom experience teaching prelicense real estate full-time. There is no one as familiar with the Oregon real estate licensing examinations as he is. Before entering the real estate field, Mr. Jeddeloh worked for a large commercial bank in Oregon and also taught public secondary schools in Oregon. Mr. Jeddeloh has an undergraduate degree in Education and did his graduate work in Business Administration, Law and Finance. Students who have taken his live instruction classes are always impressed by his ability to explain complex subjects clearly and understandably.

The author's combination of knowledge and experience have resulted in this book being the most comprehensive text available for the study of real estate agency in Oregon.

Getting a Real Estate License

Real estate brokerage is a relatively young profession compared to other professional fields such as medicine and law. Real estate agents were almost totally unregulated until 1908 when the National Association of Real Estate Boards was formed (currently the National Association of Realtors®. In fact, the chief purpose for which the National Association of Real Estate Boards was formed was to create a Code of Ethics and to encourage government licensing of real estate agents.

Even then, membership and adherence to the Code of Ethics was voluntary. Oregon led the nation by creating the first effective real estate licensing law in 1919. Today, this law is known as the Oregon Real Estate License Law, and is augmented by numerous Administrative rules promulgated by the Oregon Real Estate Agency. The Real Estate License Law requires that you hold one of several different kinds of real estate licenses in order to engage in what the law refers to as "professional real estate activity." Which kind of license you obtain depends on what kind of real estate activity you plan to do, and whether you plan to work for another agent or be independent. Most of these real estate licenses require completion of a separate license examination.

Most persons new to the real estate profession must get a brokers license as their first license. A brokers license entitles you to engage in all kinds of professional real estate activity except appraisal. (Appraisal is considered a separate field and appraisers are licensed by the Oregon Appraiser Certification and Licensure Board.) A real estate broker can work independently or cooperatively with other brokers. If you wish to run a real estate company and have other brokers working for the company, then you need a principal brokers license. With some exceptions, you cannot get a principal brokers license in Oregon without meeting additional educational requirements and having three years of experience as a broker. The most notable exceptions to these rules are for out of state licensees or for persons who have held a license in another state and now reside in Oregon. Partial or full waiver of the time requirement is also possible if you can demonstrate substantial experience related to real estate, although a full waiver is granted only in exceptional circumstances. Since each individual's situation will be unique, if you feel you might qualify for a waiver, and wish to apply directly for a brokers license, you should contact the Oregon Real Estate Agency to determine the exact requirements. Their address is: Oregon Real Estate Agency, 1177 Center Street N.E., Salem, Oregon 97310, Telephone (503) 378-4170.

Assuming, however, that you are new to the profession and do not have significant previous real estate experience, you will need to start with the regular brokers license if you wish to engage in real estate sales. If you wish to conduct property management activity, and your professional real estate activity will be limited to property management, then you may wish to consider the special property managers license (see *Property managers license* below).

There are four requirements to obtain a brokers license. You must

- Be 18 years of age,
- Be of good character,
- Demonstrate competence in Oregon Real Estate Law. Real Estate Finance, Real Estate Practices, Property Management, Real Estate Agency, Real Estate Brokerage and Real Estate Contracts, and you must
- Take and pass the national and state (Oregon) real estate brokers exams.

Since most persons have no problem with the first two requirements, let us confine our discussion to the last two.

You must demonstrate competence in the seven subject areas by taking and passing a course in each subject area in a school where the course(s) have been approved by the Oregon Real Estate Agency.

The real estate examinations consist of the Oregon exam (also called the state exam) and the national exam. These exams are always given at the same time, which is every month on the third or fourth Saturday (except La Grande test center, which is only three times a year). You must pass both exams with a score of 75% or better. If you pass one exam, but fail the other, you need to retake only the exam you failed, provided that you finally pass it within 12 months of passing the first exam.

Both exams are made up of totally objective multiple choice questions. The Oregon exam consists of 50 questions and the national exam has 150 questions. Most states now split their examinations into a state portion and a national portion (also sometimes called "multi-state" or "uniform" exam). As a result, if you ever move to another state you will usually only have to take the state portion in the new state, since most states now recognize Oregon's national exam as meeting the same requirements as their national, multi-state or uniform exam.

In order for a course to be approved by the Oregon Real Estate Agency it must meet certain requirements. In particular, a course in Oregon Real Estate Agency must cover the material presented in this text. Another requirement is that you must actually spend the time taking the course, either in a tape presentation with an instructor present, in a live classroom setting, or by approved distance education (e.g., by the internet or through correspondence).

Property managers license: In early 1988 it became possible to obtain a special license as a property manager. The requirements for the property managers license are the same as for the brokers license, except that the examinations and courses are different. To obtain a property managers license you need to demonstrate competence only in Oregon Property Management. In addition you must take a general examination on property management consisting of 100 questions. You should bear in mind that a property manager licensee is limited strictly to property management; you cannot be involved in any real estate activity that involves a sale. For example, you could lease a property to a tenant, but you could not do a lease-option because if the option is exercised it would result in a sale. Note also that brokers and principal brokers can also do property management, so if you want to be involved in both sales and property management, then the brokers license is the one to get.

Applying for the Examinations: The deadline for applying for any real estate exam is generally the fifth day of the month in which you wish to take the exam. In other words, if you want to take an exam scheduled for the third Saturday in December, you must apply no later than December 5. Note that your application must be postmarked by December 5, not received in Salem by December 5.

However, you should mail your application as soon as possible. Many test centers have limited space (especially the Portland center). If the test center you have chosen is filled when your application is received, then you will be assigned the next closest center where space is available.

The fee for the examination is $75 for the brokers national and state (or either exam separately), and the property managers exam is also $75. In addition, you must submit a fingerprint card the first time you apply to take an examination. The fingerprint card must be completed by an official qualified to take fingerprints. The Real Estate Agency charges $40 for processing the fingerprint card. The fingerprint card will be submitted to the FBI for criminal activity check. You can take the examination(s) at any time, but no license will be issued until the check is completed. This can take several months, so the fingerprint card should be submitted immediately once you have made the decision to obtain the license. You can submit the fingerprint card with the fee for processing it alone and send in the exam application later. The fingerprint card must be obtained from the Real Estate Agency; generic fingerprint cards from other agencies are not acceptable.

You may obtain an exam application, fingerprint card and *Examination Information* booklet from the Oregon Real Estate Agency (see address and phone above). These materials are also available free of charge at the most real estate schools.

Study Hints

Successful students know that if you master the terminology of a given subject area, you will have mastered that subject. This is particularly true of real estate because you will encounter an overwhelming number of new terms to learn. Don't let a new word get by you without learning its meaning and how it is used. About half the exam items are really just vocabulary questions – testing your knowledge of real estate terminology. So if you know the language of real estate thoroughly, you will have the subject well in hand at exam time. To assist you in mastering real estate vocabulary, you will find a *Key terms* section at the end of the reading in each section. Each of the key terms listed is italicized where it first appears in the preceding text, so you can easily check on its meaning and usage.

Always be sure you understand a topic thoroughly before going on to the next topic. Since you will forget material as you progress through the course, you should start a program of systematic review of the material previously studied. A wise man once said "if you want to increase your vocabulary, use a new word three times a day for three days and it will be yours forever." This works because people learn best by a sequence of learning, forgetting, relearning, forgetting, relearning, and so on. Each time you learn-forget-relearn you double the time before you will forget the material.

Another good study trick is to look for common elements and ways to tie information together. If you try to memorize facts in isolation, it is very difficult to remember them for long enough to pass an exam. But if you get an overall picture, the individual facts are easier to remember. After all, individual facts make more sense when you have a framework to place them in.

Do not be alarmed if you find your retention is poor at first. It is not uncommon for students to retain only 20-30% of the information after just one reading. But if you do not give up, you will find that successive readings (plus attendance at the lectures for which this text was designed) will increase your memory remarkably.

Exam Techniques

At the end of the first section in this text you will find various sample exam questions which are similar to the type of questions you will find on the real estate exams given by the Real Estate Agency. You should be sure you practice with these questions, as they are the most important part of the text if you are planning on taking licensing exams.

There are three basic question types. Probably the most prevalent type is the *completion* or *fill-in* type of question (see examples below). Almost as common is the *double true-false* format, and occasionally you will encounter a *Roman numeral* type of question. But regardless of the type of question, all test questions are comprised of two parts. The first part is called the **stem**, and it is the part that actually "asks the question." The stem is followed by three **distracters** or **foils**, which are the three wrong answer choices, and, of course, the correct answer.

For example, in the following question, the stem is in regular print, and the distracters or foils are underlined. The correct answer is in italics:

> In real estate, a preliminary sales contract is called
> (A) a listing agreement.
> (B) a lease-option.
> (C) *an earnest money agreement.*
> (D) an offering.

Many students make silly mistakes answering questions because they were never taught the simple ground rules for answering questions. The rules are really very easy:

1. Read the stem and the first answer (answer A) as an entire sentence. Then decide whether the statement is true or false. Using your pencil, make a notation of your decision next to the answer.

2. Read the stem again, this time followed by the second answer (answer B). Again, decide whether the statement is true or false and mark your decision next to the answer. Repeat the process for the last two answers (C and D). It is important to remember to read the stem over again each time.

3. When you have finished, the correct answer will be obvious – whichever answer is the "odd man out" is the correct answer. In other words, if you marked three answers false and one answer true, then the one marked true must be the correct answer. Similarly, with some types of negative questions, you may mark three answers true and one answer false. Then the one marked false is the correct answer.

When you finish the above question, it should look like this:

> In real estate, a preliminary sales contract is called
> *f* (A) a listing agreement.
> *f* (B) a lease-option.
> *t* (C) an earnest money agreement.
> *f* (D) an offering.

Be sure to mark your decision for each answer. Do not attempt to trust your memory. By the time you finish reading the fourth answer, you could easily have forgotten what you decided about the first answer. This technique is not only useful for avoiding silly mistakes, but also when you are not sure of the answer and must make a partial guess.

Fill-in and completion questions

These questions are really the same type of question. The only difference is that in the fill-in question an actual blank appears in the question, while the completion question contains an assumed blank at the end of the stem. For example –

> The _____ is the interest held by the vendor during the term of a land sales contract.
>
> (A) equitable title   (C) naked title
> (B) marketable title   (D) insurable title
>
> or
>
> The interest held by the vendor during the term of a land sales contract is the
>
> (A) equitable title.   (C) naked title.
> (B) marketable title.   (D) insurable title.

After you answered the above questions, your answer section should have looked like this

> *f* (A) equitable title.   *t* (C) naked title.
> *f* (B) marketable title.   *f* (D) insurable title.

The fill-in or completion format is especially useful for testing knowledge of vocabulary items. Since testing your familiarity with real estate terminology is a fundamental part of the real estate exams, you will find many fill-in and completion questions.

Double true-false questions

The second most commonly encountered exam question type is the double true-false question. These questions come in one of two formats, e.g.

According to the Real Estate License Law, the
  I. Real Estate Commissioner is the seventh member of the Real Estate Board.
  II. decisions of the Real Estate Commissioner cannot be appealed.
(A) I only   (C) Both I and II
(B) II only   (D) Neither I nor II

or sometimes the format is like this –
According to the Real Estate License Law,
(A) the Real Estate Commissioner is the seventh member of the Real Estate Board.
(B) the decisions of the Real Estate Commissioner cannot be appealed.
(C) both A and B are true.
(D) neither A nor B is true.

In answering the double true-false question, follow exactly the same rules as for the fill-in or completion question. That is, first read the stem and the first answer (Roman numeral I in the first example, and (A) in the second format). Decide whether the statement is true or false, and mark your decision next to the answer. Then read the stem again, followed by the second answer, and decide whether this statement is true or false. Again mark your decision next to the answer. When you have marked both answers, the correct choice is obvious.

Double true-false questions are popular with test makers because they are easy to write. They are hard on students, however, because if you have to guess at one of the answers, you have only a 50-50 chance.

After you have answered the above question, it should look like this:

According to the Real Estate License Law, the
t I. Real Estate Commissioner is the seventh member of the Real Estate Board.
f II. decisions of the Real Estate Commissioner cannot be appealed.
(A) I only   (C) Both I and II above
(B) II only   (D) Neither I nor II above

or
According to the Real Estate License Law,
t (A) the Real Estate Commissioner is the seventh member of the Real Estate Board.
f (B) the decisions of the Real Estate Commissioner cannot be appealed.
(C) Both A and B above are true.
(D) Neither A nor B above is true.

Roman numeral questions

A third type of question which occasionally occurs on the real estate exams is the Roman numeral question. This question is similar to the double true-false question above, but instead of having two answers (I and II), it has three or more answers. As a result, the choices (A, B, C AND D) may have a variety of choice combinations. For example –

Which of the following would be an encumbrance on a real estate title?
  I. A land sales contract
  II. An easement
  III. A trust deed
  IV. A mortgage
(A) I, III and IV only   (C) IV only
(B) III and IV only   (D) All of the above

Answer the Roman numeral question the same way as you answered the preceding question formats. That is, read the stem followed by each answer in turn and decide whether it is true or false, mark your decision, and continue until you have marked each answer. Always re-read the stem for each answer. When you have marked all the answers, you can easily select the correct answer. After you have completed the above question, the Roman numeral section should look like this –

t I. A land sales contract
t II. An easement
t III. A trust deed
t IV. A mortgage

Notice that regardless of the question format, you always mark your true-false decisions next to each answer and always re-read the stem with each answer. The importance of this technique cannot be overstressed. It is very common for students to let the first answer color their thinking about the second answer. *You cannot do this.* Each answer is distinct and separate from each other and must be considered in isolation. Making your true-false markings as you decide about each answer is the only way to ensure that you will do this properly.

Question sets

On rare occasions, you may encounter on the real estate exams a set of two or more questions which are related to each other. In other words, data from a question is referred to and used in one or more following questions. However, you will never find a set of questions where you must get the answer correct to the first one before you can get the answer correct for the following question(s). In other words, the questions may use common data, but they must be kept separate to the extent that missing a previous question will not cause you to miss a subsequent question.

Frequently, when this technique is employed, there will be a chart or graph to which a number of questions will be directed. These questions are unpopular with test makers because it becomes hard to store the questions individually and they become inflexible when trying to make up a new exam.

One situation on the real estate exams, however, does consistently make use of the question set technique. When testing your knowledge of listing agreements and earnest money receipts, the Real Estate Agency usually includes a "narrative" – that is, a story about how a transaction is to take place. The narrative is followed by a sample listing agreement or earnest money receipt. The listing agreement or earnest money receipt will contain blanks, several of which are numbered. One or more questions then follow, and each question asks what should be placed in one of the numbered blanks. Note that all the questions use the same common data (the narrative), but each question is separate and distinct from the others. That is, you can miss any one question but still have an equal opportunity to get all the others correct.

Ranking the answers

Many times, when answering a test item, you might find that you are unsure of the right answer. Since there is no penalty on the real estate exams for guessing, by all means you should answer the question. But some students have problems deciding which answer to choose. If this happens to you, it may be helpful to use a *ranking technique*, a modification of the true-false marking system discussed above. For example, suppose we had the same completion question we used previously,

The interest held by the vendor during the term of a land sales contract is the

(A) equitable title.   (C) naked title.
(B) marketable title.   (D) insurable title.

Except that this time, suppose you are not sure of the answer. Suppose that you read the stem and answer (A) and decide that it is definitely false, so you mark it false. Then you read the stem again with answer (B), and you decide that the answer is probably true. So you mark (B) as true. When you read the stem again followed by answer (C), you decide that this is a true statement also, so you mark (C) as true. Finally, you read the stem the fourth time followed by answer (D), and this time you also decide the statement is true. When you mark answer (D) as true, you are faced with a dilemma – which is the correct answer among (B), (C) and (D)? Only one answer can be true, but you answered three with true –

The interest held by the vendor during the term of a land sales contract is the

f (A) equitable title.   *t* (C) naked title.
t (B) marketable title.   *t* (D) insurable title.

The answer is to rank the ones of which you are unsure. It is usually easiest to do this in pairs. For example, ask yourself the question, "Do I like (B) better than (C)?" If you answer yourself that you like (C) better than (B), then eliminate (B) by marking it false. Next, decide between the two remaining choices, (C) and (D). Ask yourself which of these two you think is more likely to be true. If you decide (C) is more likely to be true than (D), then eliminate (D) by marking it false. By this process of elimination you have arrived at the decision that (C) is the correct answer. This method works because it is human nature to get confused when we have too many choices to make, but it is always easy to decide between just two items at a time.

Elimination technique

Sometimes you might encounter a problem where you have no idea whether any of the answers is right or not. In this situation, you might still be able to save the day. Many times you can get at the correct answer to a question by eliminating the answers you know are not correct. If you can eliminate three answers as definitely wrong, then you know the fourth answer has to be the correct one.

Use your subconscious mind

Another trick used by successful test takers is to exert a reluctance to change their answers. Good students know that the subconscious mind is a powerful force. They know that they may not be able consciously to remember the answer, but if they ever read the information in the past it is still stored somewhere in their unconscious mind. Therefore, a good rule of thumb when guessing is to stick by your first answer. Of course, when checking over your test at the end you may discover that you completely misunderstood the question, in which case you are certainly justified in changing your answer.

Work the answers backwards

There is another clever technique which is very useful for certain difficult math questions. While the math questions on the real estate exams are a lot easier than many people fear, still there may occasionally be a math problem that is especially difficult. For example, look at the following problem —

A seller told an agent that she wanted to net $160,000 from the sale of her lot, which she felt had a market value of about $180,000. She told the agent that the agent could have everything over the $160,000 as commission. However, the agent did not wish to take a listing on this basis, and decided to list it at a set price which would include the amount the seller wished to net plus a commission of 6%. At what price should the agent list?

(A) $160,000   (C) $170,213
(B) $169,600   (D) $180,000

Now, the way to calculate this correctly is to divide the $160,000 the seller wishes to net by 94%. This is because $160,000 is 94% of what the agent needs to list the property for. However, if you cannot remember how to do the problem, you can still get the right answer another way.

Obviously, one of the four answers above is correct. So you can figure out which is the correct answer just by calculating which one works. Take your calculator, subtract 6% of each answer from that answer in turn, until you find the answer that will leave you with $160,000. As you can see, this technique can make stubborn math problems a breeze.

Learn to smell the answers

Good test takers are usually people who have taken a lot of standardized tests and therefore have come to understand these principles. They have also developed a second sense — they almost seem to be able to "smell" wrong answers put in deliberately to mislead them. The best way for you to develop this second sense is to practice, practice, practice. Go over each and every sample test question without fail.

One thing you can do which will help you develop this second sense is to watch out for key words in a question. Pay particular attention to negative words such as *not, least, except,* and so forth. Also pay close attention to words such as *never* and *always.* In the real world, things are seldom absolute, so answers containing the words *never* and *always* tend to be untrue.

Pay attention also to the grammatical flow of the question. If there seems to be an abrupt change when you leave the stem and start reading the answer, this can be a clue that the answer is not true. On the other hand, answers which are long, wordy or full of qualifications tend to be true statements. Of course, all of this advice can really only be useful in those cases where you are reduced to guessing anyway. If you know the material, you won't need to worry about second-guessing the test makers.

Choosing the best answer

Many students complain that the test questions seem to have more than one correct answer. They report that one answer may be better than another, but it confuses them when two or more answers are both technically correct. In reality, students who find more than one correct answer are students who really do not understand the material thoroughly. In fact, very few questions have two correct answers and force you to choose the better of the two. The fact is that students who have learned some of the material, but not all of it, find they are able to discriminate down to the last two choices, both of which sound correct to them. But if they knew the material better, they would realize that only one of these last two is really correct.

Incomplete answers

Don't let an incomplete statement fool you. For example, suppose you read the stem of a question and the first answer and it reads "For a valid escrow to exist, there must be: (A) an escrow agent and escrow instructions." You immediately conclude that this is a false statement, because there are several other requirements to create a valid escrow in addition to "an escrow agent and escrow instructions." Wrong! If you read the statement all by itself, it is a true statement, because an escrow agent and escrow instructions are required for a valid escrow. The fact that there are other requirements is irrelevant to the truth of this statement.

Don't "what if" the question

One of the most common mistakes students make is to add material or facts to a question that is not stated. People tend to jump to conclusions and make unwarranted assumptions. This can lead to errors. Consider the following question –

> An office manager has assigned all the leads during one afternoon to Hans Schmidt, a broker licensed with the company. Consuelo Moreno, another of the company's brokers is also in the office at the same time. In the middle of the afternoon, Mr. and Mrs. Gomez come in to inquire about buying a property. If the manager assigns the buyers to Moreno,
>
> (A) this is steering.
> (B) the broker has violated the Fair Housing Act.
> (C) both A and B above are correct.
> (D) neither A nor B above is correct.

The correct answer is (C), because assigning clients to brokers on the basis of race, religion, national origin, sex, mental or physical handicap or familial status (having children), is a called *steering* and is a violation of the Fair Housing Act. But many students read this question and add the assumption that the Gomez' do not speak English. Then they add the assumption that the Gomez' do speak Spanish, that Schmidt does not speak Spanish, and that Moreno does speak Spanish! Notice that the stem and the answers do not address the language issue at all, so you must assume that everyone speaks English.

Do the easy questions first

You can maximize your probability of success if you do not let the difficult questions slow you down. If you are taking the national and Oregon exams, you will have almost two whole minutes per question. Since most questions won't take more than about 30 seconds, this will be plenty of time. But if you spend 15 minutes on one tough question, and as a result lack time to finish all of the easy questions, you will be the loser.

To avoid this, the best technique is to answer all the easy questions first. Leave the more difficult questions for a second pass later. After you have finished the easy ones, you will find that you have lots of time left to go back and do the harder ones. Furthermore, you will be more relaxed, more mentally conditioned to the test, and you may have found some material which jogged your memory about one of the harder questions you skipped earlier. Some students still skip some of the especially difficult questions on their second pass and save them for a third pass later. If you follow this approach, you can be sure that, if you run out of time,

the questions you didn't have time to finish were the questions you had the least chance of getting right anyway.

Double-check your work

When you finally finish the exam, make a final double-check of your work. Don't forget to check your answer sheet — remember that you get no credit for the right answer unless it is clearly marked with pencil in the proper place on the answer sheet. If you skip a question, be especially careful to place your answers in the right space on the answer sheet. Also be sure that your name and other information is correct. When students talk over the exam afterwards with other students, they usually realize that they made at least one, stupid, silly mistake. In fact, the average error rate is about one silly mistake per 50 exam questions, even when you are trying your best to be careful. If you have time remaining, check your work over carefully; this is no time to get sloppy.

Get ahead of the game

As the day for the exam draws near, you will quite naturally feel nervous and apprehensive. This is really a senseless time for you to feel this way! If you studied well, then you are as prepared to take the exams as any of the other people you will meet at the test center. If you haven't done your work by now, well, it's probably too late anyway. So whether you are prepared or not, it makes no sense to worry. The best course of action for the last couple of days before the exams is to continue to review and study, but *relax*! Of course, it also helps to get plenty of rest, watch your diet, and don't let the rest of the world get in your way, but the most important factor is to stay relaxed.

Make your final preparations for the exam several days in advance. Since you may have to drive some distance, be sure to set the alarm clock early enough. Also tend to other mundane matters such as getting together your pencils, admission ticket, identification, calculator (don't forget fresh batteries), and even fill up the car with gas. Get your family to help you for the last couple of days by taking the rest of your usual chores off your back to allow you time to review in peace and quiet. If you can do all this, you can sit down to take the exam feeling confident that you are as prepared as it is possible to be and that ***nothing is going to stand in the way of your success!***

THE LAW OF AGENCY

A LTHOUGH REAL ESTATE AGENTS MUST BE CONVERSANT WITH MANY LAWS, THE most important is the law of agency, for it is the law of agency that governs the day to day relationships that the agent forms with sellers, buyers, and practically everyone the agent comes in contact with.

The law of agency is not unique to real estate – there are many fields in which the law of agency is important. We are all familiar with travel agents, insurance agents, entertainers' agents, among others. All of these agents operate under much the same set of rules as real estate agents.

As a generalization, an ***agent*** is one who is authorized to represent the interests of another (called a ***principal***) in negotiations or dealings with third parties. Because there is always a principal as well as the agent, the ***law of agency*** is frequently called the law of ***principal and agent***.

There are two central concepts in practically any agency relationship. One is that the principal relies on the agent as an expert for specialized advice. The other is that the agent has a high standard of responsibility toward the principal's best interests. This responsibility is called the agent's ***fiduciary*** duty to the principal.

The key idea in the agency relationship is the authority. The agent is simply someone to whom the principal has given authority. In fact, the whole purpose of the law of agency is to allow people to expand the scope of their activity. Because of the law of agency, you can hire unlimited numbers of persons to represent you, and even to enter into contracts on your behalf with third parties. And if you authorize your agent to hire his or her own agents, the number of people representing you can multiply indefinitely. You can see that the law of agency creates endless possibilities.

An easy way to look at agency is to examine a common agency relationship that most people are familiar with – a power of attorney. If you give someone a power of attorney, you become the principal, and you give the other party authority to do something on your behalf, such as signing a document for you. The party you authorize is called an *attorney in fact* (as opposed to an attorney at law). The attorney in fact is your agent and you will be bound by the document he or she signed on your behalf provided, of course, that the attorney in fact acted within the scope of the authority you granted.

Now that we have a basic grasp of the purpose of the law of agency, let us turn our attention to its real estate application. If an agent is one who is authorized to represent another, and sometimes authorized to enter into a contract with another on behalf of a principal, then in a typical real estate transaction, who is the principal and who is the agent? The answer is not simple. In a traditional sale of real estate, the seller lists the property with the broker. In effect, the seller hires the broker as an agent. Therefore, the seller is the principal, the broker is the agent, and the broker has a fiduciary duty to the seller.

Nevertheless, it is perfectly possible for the broker to represent the buyer, although the majority represent sellers. And, of course, in other types of real estate activity, brokers represent different parties. In property management, brokers and property managers commonly represent owners in their negotiations with renters and lessees. Here again, while brokers and property managers would most likely represent the owner, it is also perfectly possible for them to represent a potential tenant. We will discuss the issue of buyer brokerage and tenant brokerage in more detail later.

So far we have discussed only the role of the owner's agent, i.e., the broker or property manager. But brokers may hire other brokers or property manager licensees, and a property manager licensee who is acting independently may hire other property managers. What happens if the broker hires another broker or a property manager hires another property manager? Then the broker or property manager who acts as the employee of a broker or property manager, becomes the agent of the employing broker or property manager. As we noted above, the principal can authorize the agent to hire his or her own agents, and this is precisely what happens in a most real estate transactions – the owner hires the broker or property manager as an agent, and grants the broker or property manager the authority to hire other persons as agents for the broker or property manager. The broker or property manager then hires other brokers and/or other property managers as agents of the broker. The broker's or property manager's employees in this situation are frequently referred to as subagents. Subagency will also be covered in greater detail later.

Many agents use the words *client* and *customer* with special meanings. Agents commonly refer to the principal as a client, and to third parties (usually buyers) as customers. While these are not legal definitions, and not all agents use them as we have defined them here, these are nevertheless common definitions.

Types of agents

As we noted above, you become an agent when the principal grants you *authority*. The authority may be to represent the principal in a single task, various tasks, or may even be unlimited authority.

An agent who is given authority to represent the principal for just one task is called a *special agent*. Most of the time real estate brokers act as special agents. For example, a seller will hire the broker to sell the property. This is just one task.

An agent who is given various or several tasks, or more commonly, a category of tasks, is a *general agent*. Property managers, for example, would be general agents, since the owner gives them authority to show and rent vacant property, arrange for repairs and maintenance, make mortgage payments, and take care of many other matters relating to their investment. In the case of the property manager, the owner grants the agent authority for the entire category of tasks, so it is a general agency. The relationship between a broker and employee brokers is another example. The broker gives the employees the authority to handle any of the properties the broker has listed, including showing property, writing offers and getting them accepted, the authority to take new listings, possibly the authority to engage in property management, and so on. Since this is a category of tasks, the agency is general.

An agent who is granted unlimited authority is called a ***universal agent***. An unlimited power of attorney would be a common example of a universal agency. Guardians and conservators of minors and incompetents are also usually universal agents. A universal agent in real estate would be rare.

Exercise a

An agent is someone who represents a _____ . The agent has a _____ duty to the _____ and is generally required to have specialized knowledge. The relationship is normally created when the _____ gives the agent _____ . Someone who signs a document for another is an _____ _____ _____ , and is operating under a _____ _____ _____ , a type of agency agreement. When a _____ agreement is taken, the agent represents the seller. In real estate sales, it is also common today for the agent to represent the _____ . Most real estate agents refer to their _____ as a _____ . An agent who is given just one task is a _____ agent. If an agent is granted authority to perform a category of tasks, the agency is _____ . When an agent has been granted unlimited authority, then we say it is a _____ agency.

Special income tax considerations

Although not properly a discussion of agency, mention must be made of the issue of withholding taxes. Under the Internal Revenue Code, wages, salaries and the like are subject to withholding, and the employer is subject to certain payroll taxes. Of course, regardless of whether or not there is withholding, if you earn money you must pay tax on it. The issue is whether your broker withholds for your income taxes, or whether there is no withholding and you pay your taxes yourself. Note that, even if there is no withholding, in most cases you will have to file and pay estimated taxes quarterly. But at least, without withholding, you get the use of the money until filing time. It also simplifies the bookkeeping for a broker or property manager who employs subagents. In the Internal Revenue Code, taxpayers whose income is subject to withholding are called ***employees***. Taxpayers whose income is not subject to withholding are called ***independent contractors***.

NOTES

Real estate agents have zealously guarded their right to be independent contractors. In the past, the Internal Revenue Service attacked this right at every opportunity. As a result Realtors® lobbied Congress for clarification of this issue. The outcome was the "Safe Harbor Rules" which have been made a part of the Internal Revenue Code. Under the Safe Harbor Rules, a real estate agent (including a property manager) is an independent contractor for federal tax purposes if several conditions exist:

- The agent is a real estate licensee,
- The agent's income is almost entirely based on production rather than on hours worked, i.e., the agent's income is at risk,
- The agent provides at least some of the materials and equipment required (e.g., an automobile), and
- There is a written contract which specifies that the agent is an independent contractor and not an employee.

In real estate sales today, practically all agents act as independent contractors. In other types of real estate activity, such as property management, commercial leasing, appraisal and the like, most agents are still independent contractors, but it is less unusual to find employees.

Exercise b

If your income is subject to withholding taxes, then you are an _____ under the Internal Revenue Code. The income of _____ _____ is not subject to withholding. You are generally an _____ _____ if you and your employer follow the Safe Harbor Rules.

Agent's compensation

An agent's compensation is determined strictly by negotiation with the principal. There is no set fee. If any organization set fees it would be in restraint of trade and a violation of anti-trust laws, both state and federal.

However, an individual broker may set his or her own standards. And a real estate brokerage firm may set minimums for the company which all brokers working for the company must adhere to. What is illegal is if one real estate company conspires with other companies to set minimum fees. To avoid claims of price fixing most real estate companies instruct their brokers never even to discuss company fee policies with brokers from other companies.

Creating agency relationships

An agency relationship is created when the principal grants the agent authority, as we have seen above. At first blush this would simply appear to be an ordinary contract. Yet the agency relationship is not contractual in the strict sense of the word. A better term to describe it would be "consensual," since it is derived from the consent of the principal. Also, unlike most contracts, consideration is not required to create an agency relationship.

There are three ways that agency relationships are normally created. The most common is where the consent to be represented is stated orally or in writing, in which case we say it is an **expressed agency**. If the agency involves real estate, the **Statute of Frauds** requires it to be in writing and to state the agent's compensation with reasonable certainty, lest it be void. Besides listing agreements, typical agency contracts in real estate include property management agreements, appraisal orders, buyer brokerage agreements, escrow instructions, and the like. Note that an earnest money agreement is not an agency agreement. The only real estate contracts that are agency contracts are those where someone hires someone else to provide a service.

An agency can also be created where the principal agrees to the agent's actions after the agent has acted. In this case, we say the agency was created by **ratification**, that is, that the principal ratified the agency. For example, suppose you know an owner wishes to sell his or her real estate, but has not yet given anyone a listing agreement. Suddenly you have a prospective buyer who might be interested in the property, but there is no time to go to the owner and obtain a listing agreement prior to showing it, so you show it to the prospective buyer anyway, without an expressed agency. After showing it to the prospect, you have time to contact the owner and obtain the owner's consent for you to represent the owner. If you obtain the owner's consent after performing the task, the owner is now bound by the fact that you are his or her agent, retroactively to the beginning of the act.

The previous example can also serve to illustrate another point about ratification. Suppose you were able to secure an offer from the prospective buyer and the owner were to accept the offer. It is fundamental in agency law that when a principal accepts the benefit of the agent's actions, the principal ratifies those actions, even though there was no expressed ratification. In other words, the principal cannot accept the benefit of your actions as his or her agent without recognizing you as an authorized agent.

Since an agency relationship frequently involves many authorities, it sometimes occurs that only one particular authority is ratified, the rest having been expressed. For example, suppose you take a listing agreement on a property (creating an expressed agency), but in the agreement the owner insists that there be no sign on the property. However, you proceed to place a sign on the property anyway. Since this exceeds your authority, this action could have dire consequences, as we will discuss later. But if the owner then agrees that the sign can stay, the owner ratifies your authority to place a sign on the property. Similarly, if the sign produces a buyer and the owner knows you put the sign on the property, and the owner accepts the offer from the buyer, then the owner has accepted the benefit of the wrongful action, and is thereby deemed to have ratified the authority.

Less commonly, an agency is sometimes created where one party leads someone to believe that an agency exists. Under the right circumstances, this can result in an **agency by estoppel**. We call it an agency by estoppel because the party who led the other to believe an agency exists is estopped (barred) from denying the existence of the agency.

For example, suppose a property owner allows a friend to take care of various business matters such as writing checks to pay the owner's bills, purchasing supplies on behalf of the owner, and so on. A broker knows that the friend has done these things for the owner over a period of time. The friend (not the owner) then gives the broker an agreement to secure a buyer for the owner's property. In good faith, the broker shows the property to a prospective buyer and secures an offer to buy, which the owner then accepts. Must the owner pay the brokerage fee? Assuming that a court would agree that the broker had the right to rely on the circumstances, the owner would be estopped from denying that the friend was authorized to act on the owner's behalf. An agency by estoppel was created.

A common agency created by estoppel occurs where an owner has not hired the agent formally, but nevertheless allows the agent to show the owner's property to a potential buyer. If the owner takes no action to correct the impression of the buyer that the agent is authorized, then the agency becomes established and both the agent and the third party may rely upon it.

This can be even more direct, such as where the owner leads the agent to believe that the agent is authorized to represent the owner. In this case, however, the agent will have a more difficult time collecting compensation because the owner can raise the defense of the Statute of Frauds, which requires agency agreements in Oregon to be in writing and state the compensation with reasonable certainty .

An important point about agencies created by estoppel is that either party can create the belief in the other. In other words, the owner can lead an agent to believe that the owner authorizes the agent, thus creating an agency by estoppel. But in similar fashion, the agent can lead the owner to believe that the agent is representing the owner, in which case an agency has also been created by estoppel. Or an agent could lead a third party to believe the agent was representing the third party, such as where a real estate agent leads a prospective buyer to believe that the agent is representing the buyer. These are sometimes referred to as ***accidental*** or ***unintentional agencies***. Creating an accidental agency with the buyer can have far-reaching implications when the broker is already representing the owner under an expressed listing agreement. These problems will be discussed in more detail later.

The scope of the agent's authority is usually expressed in the agreement which creates the agency. For example, a listing agreement for a home would likely grant the agent authority to show the property, to place a for sale sign on the property, to advertise the property, to hire additional agents (other brokers), to cooperate with brokers in other real estate companies, and the like. However, an owner may not wish a sign, or may wish to withhold some other authority. This is generally accomplished simply by modifying the standard listing agreement form.

Property management agreements usually present a completely different set of authorities to the agent than you find in real estate sales. Where a listing agreement for the sale of a property would authorize the agent to secure offers, it would generally not authorize the agent to accept the buyer's offer on behalf of the seller. Of course, it is possible for a listing to grant the agent the authority to accept an offer, but most agents would feel that such authority might create more liability than the agent cares to accept. In property management agreements, however, the agent usually does accept the authority to enter into contracts with third parties (tenants) on behalf of the owner. A property management contract might typically authorize the agent to set rental rates, advertise the property for rent or lease, show the property, take applications from tenants, check credit and other references and make credit decisions, and then enter into rental agreements on behalf of the owner.

As you can see, the agency contract usually contains extensive provisions expressing the authority of the agent. All such provisions are called ***expressed actual authority***. But there is almost always another kind of authority that is created. Where the listing, buyer service agreement, property management agreement, or other document creates all sorts of specific authorities, it can never express every detail or conceivable circumstance that might occur during the agent's performance of the agreement. For example, a listing contract may stipulate that the agent may show the property during reasonable hours, but it may not stipulate what hours are reasonable, or whether the agent is authorized to use the agent's personal automobile to bring the prospective buyers to the property, and so forth. Nevertheless, even though these authorities are not expressed, they are ***implied***. The law refers to such authority as ***implied actual authority***, defined as the authority which is necessary to the performance of the expressed authority.

In addition to expressed and implied actual authority, the law also recognizes **apparent** or **ostensible authority**. This is the authority granted when the agency is created by estoppel.

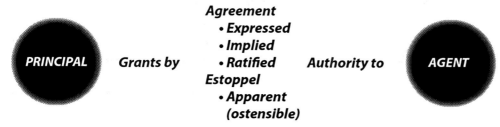

PRINCIPAL   Grants by   Agreement
                                        • *Expressed*
                                        • *Implied*
                                        • *Ratified*   Authority to   AGENT
                                      Estoppel
                                        • *Apparent*
                                        (ostensible)

The usual ways in which an agency can be created

Another important point about agency relationships is that the principal is liable to third parties for the actions of the agent when the agent is acting within the scope of the authority granted by the principal, whether the authority is expressed or implied. For example, suppose a broker takes a listing agreement from an owner where the owner authorizes the broker to say something about the property in advertising the property to buyers. If the owner has specifically authorized the ad, then the owner is liable for any misrepresentations.

However, when a third party (such as a buyer) deals with an agent, the third party is required to make a reasonable attempt to determine the scope of the agent's authority. Since the third party can only hold the principal to representations and actions of the agent if the agent was acting within the scope of the agent's authority, then knowledge of the agent's authority is crucial to the third party. Courts also generally recognize disclaimers in contracts where the principal agrees to be responsible for representations made by the agent only if the representations are contained in the contract. This is called the legal principal of **respondeat superior** (let the employer respond).

What would be the penalty to the agent if the agent should exceed the authority granted by the principal? There are various liabilities the agent would incur, depending on the circumstances. For one, if the agent exceeds the authority granted by the principal, it gives the principal just cause to revoke the authority and cancel the agency agreement. As we shall see later, a principal may always revoke the authority, but if the principal revokes the authority without just cause, the agent can hold the principal liable for damages. However, if the agent has exceeded the authority granted by the principal then the principal has just cause to revoke the authority without liability for damages.

If the principal suffers a loss as a result of the agent having exceeded the agent's authority, then the principal has cause for damages. For example, suppose the agent takes an agreement to sell the principal's office building. The principal stipulates that there be no sign on the property. However, the agent places a for sale sign on the property anyway. Unknown to the agent, the principal was negotiating with a potential tenant. The tenant sees the for sale sign suddenly appear, and decides to break off negotiations. The principal has lost the tenant and the agent could be held liable for the principal's losses.

If the agent exceeds the authority granted by the principal, and as a result a third party is damaged, then the third party may have cause of action against the agent. For example, suppose a broker takes a management agreement from the owner to manage the owner's building. But the owner insists that the owner alone will sign any leases; the agent will not have the right to sign leases with prospective tenants. The agent locates a prospective tenant and wrongfully signs a lease with the tenant. In reliance on the

NOTES

agent's apparent authority, the tenant purchases furniture and moves into the premises. When the owner discovers what has happened, the owner refuses to acknowledge the lease. Since the agent acted outside of the scope of the authority granted by the owner, the tenant cannot enforce the lease on the owner. However, the tenant has cause to recover damages from the agent.

Of course, another potential liability to the agent who exceeds his or her authority is loss of the agent's real estate license. And finally, an agent who exceeds his or her authority also loses the right to collect the agent's compensation.

Exercise c

The basis of an agency relationship is the _____ which the principal grants to the agent. If granted orally or in writing, it is an _____ agency. The agency can also be _____ , as where the agent is presumed to have certain powers. We create an agency by _____ when the principal grants the _____ after the agent has performed. Agency agreements can also be created by _____ , such as in a case where one party leads another to believe there exists an agency. Then we say the authority is _____ or _____ . If the agent exceeds the agent's authority, then the _____ has just cause to _____ the authority without paying the agent the _____ . The principal, or a damaged third party could also sue the agent for _____ if the agent exceeds his or her authority. Exceeding your authority is also a violation of the Oregon _____ _____ _____ _____ , so you could also lose your license.

Agent's fiduciary obligations

As we mentioned earlier, the agent has a fiduciary duty to the principal. This fiduciary duty includes various obligations. At the top of the list we could place ***loyalty***. In fact, we could go further and say "utmost loyalty," since the agent must be loyal to the principal to the exclusion of all other interests, including the interests of the agent. That is to say, if there is a conflict between the interests of the principal and the interests of the agent, the interests of the principal come first.

And clearly, the interests of the principal also come ahead of the interests of third parties. Normally, when the agent takes a listing agreement from the owner the agent cannot also represent the prospective buyer, since the agent cannot advocate both positions at the same time. An exception occurs in a dual agency, which we will discuss later.

The agent's duty of loyalty includes the obligation of ***confidentiality***. Obviously, if the agent is to be loyal to the principal the agent cannot disclose confidential information to a third party if the information would be harmful to the position of the principal. The obligation of confidentiality goes further than just not disclosing sensitive information to the other side. It should be viewed more in the same sense that a doctor or attorney must maintain confidentiality – i.e., private matters should not be disclosed to anyone unless there is authority to do so.

In addition to loyalty, an agent owes the principal a duty of ***full disclosure***. On its face, the obligation of full disclosure would seem to be a direct contradiction to the obligation of confidentiality. But we are dealing with different matters – we must keep the principal's affairs confidential from third parties; but we must make full disclosure to the principal of anything we know about the third party. Full disclosure to the principal includes matters such as

- The fair market value of the property,
- Any relationship the agent has with third parties,
- A prospective buyer's financial condition (if representing a seller),
- That a fee will be paid to another broker or property manager,
- All offers and counteroffers as soon as received,
- If there is a deposit or earnest money, what kind (cash, check, etc.),
- The legal provisions of any offer, and

Any other material fact.

The agent could even be held responsible for disclosing facts which the agent should have known, even if the agent did not actually know. This would include matters which the broker, with the broker's special expertise should be aware of, such as matters of law relating to provisions of the earnest money agreement, local housing and zoning codes, etc.

Suppose the agent wishes to buy the property that the agent has listed. Obviously, real estate agents have the right to buy property the same as anyone else. But when the agent is the third party as well as the agent, then the agent clearly has a duty to disclose that fact to the principal. Using someone else as a ***straw man*** to keep the principal from knowing that the real party of interest is the agent is a clear violation of the law of agency. It would also be a violation of the Real Estate License Law. Similarly, any ***secret profit*** the agent makes at the expense of the principal is a violation of the agent's fiduciary obligations to the principal and of the Real Estate License Law.

The agent also owes the principal a duty of ***obedience***. Naturally, this does not mean that the agent may break the law, even if the principal instructs the agent to do so. For example, if the owner knows of a material defect in the property, this must be disclosed to the prospective buyer. Failure to disclose a material fact is fraud. Therefore, if the owner instructs the agent to keep quiet about the defect, the agent need not keep quiet and, in fact, must disclose it to the prospective buyer.

In cases where the agency itself is dependent upon following illegal instructions of the principal, the agent may not accept the agency. However, where a legitimate agency relationship exists, and thereafter the principal gives the agent illegal instructions, the agent is not required to withdraw from the agency (although doing so may be wise). In this case, the agent may continue as the principal's agent, as long as the agent refuses to obey the illegal instructions. For example, if an owner, when giving an agent a listing agreement, stipulates that the agent is not to show the property to minorities, the agent must refuse the entire agency agreement. But if the principal has already given the agent an ordinary listing agreement, and later instructs the agent to discriminate illegally, the agency may continue – the agent merely ignores the illegal instructions.

The principal is also entitled to a ***complete accounting*** for all funds and property coming into the agent's possession on behalf of the principal. In a sale transaction this is normally accomplished when the closing statement is given to the owner. In cases where deposits or other funds are collected but the transaction falls through (i.e., no final closing statement), the principal is still entitled to a complete accounting.

Not only must the agent make a complete accounting, the agent must also follow accepted practices with principal's funds and property. Mixing the principal's funds with the agent's own funds is called ***commingling***, and is a violation of the Real Estate License

Law. If the agent goes so far as to use the funds for his or her own purposes, this is called **conversion**. Either usually results in immediate revocation of the agent's license.

The agent's fiduciary responsibilities to the principal also include a duty of **due diligence**. There are many aspects to due diligence. First, the agent should not accept tasks for which the agent does not possess the necessary skills and abilities. Due diligence implies that the agent has enough knowledge of real property and related laws to advise the principal to seek the advice of appropriate counsel when necessary to protect the interests of the principal. Due diligence also includes the agent's obligation to investigate to discover material facts which affect the interests of the principal. And, of course, real estate agents are expected to have an expert knowledge of values and marketing methods.

In addition to having the ability to perform the task with reasonable care and skill, the agent must exert his or her best efforts to perform the task quickly and efficiently. An agent who fails to work on the property in the usual fashion – signs, normal advertising, showing the property – as appropriate to the property and the task assigned, is surely in violation of the obligation of due diligence to the principal.

If an agent fails to honor the agent's fiduciary obligations to the principal the consequences can be severe. Such failure is a **tort** (civil wrong) which entitles the principal to recover from the agent any damages the principal has suffered. In addition, it is just cause for the principal to revoke the authority without being liable to the agent for the agent's compensation. And it could result in revocation or suspension of the agent's license, or official reprimand.

Exercise d

The agent's fiduciary obligations to the principal include utmost _____ . *This means that the agent must keep the best interests of the principal ahead of all others, including the interests of the* _____ . *Also, the agent must not* _____ *confidential matters to anyone without authority from the principal. The agent owes the principal a duty of* _____ _____ *as well. This means that a listing agent must* _____ *certain matters to the principal such as the* _____ *of the property, the* _____ _____ *of the prospective buyer, any* _____ *the agent has with third parties, and any other* _____ *fact. The agent must also* _____ *the principal, but not to the point of breaking the law. The agent must also give the principal a complete* _____ . *And the agent must exercise* _____ _____ . *This means that the agent cannot accept tasks for which he or she does not have the necessary* _____ , *and should perform tasks as quickly and efficiently as possible. The agent's failure to honor his or her fiduciary obligations is a* _____ *which could subject the agent to suit for* _____ *or loss of the agent's real estate* _____ . *In addition the principal has just grounds to revoke the authority without being liable to the agent for the* _____ *due the agent.*

Obligations of the agent to third parties

In a traditional real estate agency relationship the broker or property manager is the agent of the property owner and owes a duty to the owner as the owner's fiduciary. This is the same whether the agent was hired to sell the property or to manage it for the owner. But even though the agent owes a fiduciary duty to the owner as the principal, the agent still has obligations to other parties in the transaction.

An agent representing the owner owes the prospective buyer or tenant an obligation of honesty, good faith, fair dealing, competence and full disclosure. Of these duties, the most common failure lies in failure to disclose. In Oregon it is considered unlawful trade practice (Unfair Trade Practices, ORS 646.608) if anyone makes any kind of false representation about real property. The statute states that the false representation may be "any assertion by words or conduct, including but not limited to, a failure to disclose a fact." (The relevant sections of the Unfair Trade Practices Act are reproduced in the Appendix.)

In addition, the 1993 Oregon Legislative Session enacted a bill that requires sellers of residential property to give buyers a detailed disclosure statement. This law applies to sales only, not rentals and leases. Nevertheless, it would also be good practice for property managers to make disclosures about the condition of the property to prospective tenants. (See Seller Property Disclosure later in this section.)

Of course, not absolutely every fact must be disclosed. The law only requires that material facts be disclosed. A material fact is some matter that would make an ordinary offeror make a different offer or not offer at all if he or she knew the truth. Even if an ordinary party would not feel some particular matter to be a material fact, if the prospective buyer or tenant asks about it, it is generally regarded as material. For example, suppose you are showing a home to a potential buyer. There is a cherry tree in the back yard. You fail to mention to the buyer that the tree produces sour pie cherries, not a table variety. To an ordinary buyer, this is probably not sufficient to be a legal cause of action. But if the buyer asks what kind of cherries it produces, the type of cherry just became a material fact, since it is obviously important to the buyer.

Not only must the matter be a material fact to be actionable at law, but in general, it must also be a latent defect. A latent defect is a matter which is hidden from view. If the plaster is falling off the walls, this is clearly a defect, and probably a material fact. But, unless the buyer is blind or buys sight unseen, the matter is not latent, since it is plainly obvious. Latent defects typically involve matters such as cesspools and septic tanks, or whether or not the property is connected to a sewer, faulty wiring, failure of a builder to build according to code, etc.

A more difficult matter is the possibility that there are conditions which should give the agent reason to suspect that something is wrong. When such conditions exist, it is not adequate for the agent to ignore the problem. Further investigation is required. Full disclosure of defects include not only matters which the agent knows, but also matters which the agent could and should have known.

The law recognizes three levels of false statements. The most serious is *fraud*. Fraud occurs where someone knew the truth and deliberately stated otherwise, or deliberately withheld the truth when there was a duty to disclose. Fraud is also a criminal act and is grounds for immediate revocation of a license.

Less serious is *negligent misrepresentation*. Negligent misrepresentation occurs where the agent made a false statement because the agent did not properly check the facts first. Negligent misrepresentation is not a criminal matter and will usually result in loss of a license only if it is a continual pattern of behavior.

Innocent misrepresentation occurs where the agent repeated information from a source ordinarily deemed to be reliable, but the information was incorrect. The classic example of innocent misrepresentation is the case where the owner fails to tell the agent of a *material latent defect* in the property. In good faith, the agent fails to disclose the defect to the buyer, because, of course, the agent did not know about it. The agent cannot generally be held responsible for innocent misrepresentations. However, the buyer may have cause of action against the owner in this case, since the owner had a duty to disclose and failed in that duty.

Fraud, negligent misrepresentation and innocent misrepresentation are referred to as *actual* when the party making the representation makes a statement orally or in writing to the other party. They are considered *constructive* when there is a duty to disclose, but no disclosure is made (fraud or misrepresentation by silence). The usual remedy is a suit for damages for the cost to repair, or for the difference between the amount paid and the market value as is. If the agent was the cause of the misrepresentation, then the principal is not required to pay the agent the agreed upon compensation.

Another possible remedy is a suit for rescission of the purchase agreement or lease. A *rescission* requires all parties to be placed in the same position they were in before they entered into the contract, as far as possible. This means that everyone must give everything back. Even the agent must return the commission to the owner, assuming that the misrepresentation was the fault of the agent.

If a third party wishes to bring action against an agent for misrepresentation, the third party must be prepared to prove that

- The agent misrepresented or failed to disclose,
- The matter was latent,
- The matter was a material fact,
- The third party relied upon the misrepresentation or failure to disclose, and
- The third party suffered damages as a result.

Probably the best way for agents to protect themselves is to shift the burden to the principal. While not a guaranteed safeguard, if the agent takes a detailed disclosure statement from the principal; a statement which clearly stipulates the condition of the land, the structure and all of its components, and all other matters relating to the property, then the agent's failure to disclose will usually be innocent (see "Seller property disclosure," later in this section). However, even if the principal makes a misrepresentation to the agent, the agent will be held responsible if the matter was something which the agent should have verified. This also includes items which appear suspicious, since the agent has a duty to inquire. The agent will also be held responsible for matters which the agent knows the principal could not or did not know about.

Exercise e

Even though the agent's _____ obligation is to the principal, the agent has a duty of _____

_____ , honesty, good faith and competence to others. A _____ is when someone

makes a false statement or fails to disclose a latent _____ _____ , yet the party knew

the truth at the time. If the party was ignorant of the truth, it is a _____ . A negligent

_____ occurs when the party should have verified a fact and did not. An innocent

_____ *occurs when the agent made a false statement but did so in reliance on a reasonable source of information. These are called _____ when the statement is made to the third party, and they are called _____ when the party is silent, but had a duty to disclose. Failure to disclose, regardless of the level, can result in a suit for _____ or for _____ of the contract. In addition, the agent could lose his or her real estate _____ if the failure to disclose was negligent or fraudulent.*

Statutory obligations of the agent

Until very recently the preceding common law fiduciary obligations of agents to their principals is all the guidance the law gave real estate brokers. However, starting in 1993 the Real Estate License Act has specified certain duties that agents have towards their clients and customers.

It is important to understand the difference between common law and statutory law. **Common law** is derived from court decisions. Based on the legal principle of precedence, once a court renders a decision in a case, the next time the same situation arises, the court must render the same decision. Today, Oregon courts rely on decisions of courts of appeal and the U.S. and Oregon Supreme Courts. These decisions are generally referred to as **landmark cases**.

Statutes, in contrast, are written by elected bodies, such as Congress, state legislatures, and even county commissioners and city councils. We write a statute when the public wishes to modify common law. The courts may change the common law by rendering new decisions, but the process is slow and not always a direct reflection of the democratic process. Of course, once the legislature writes a statute the courts have the authority to interpret it and occasionally even declare it unconstitutional.

Many times a statute will be created that gives a government agency or commissioner the authority to make **administrative rules**. Such statutes are called **enabling statutes**. Since administrative rules are not created by a democratic process they must be created following statutory requirements of publication, public input, and sometimes a public hearing before they take effect. Administrative rules must be authorized by a statute and cannot be used to amend or nullify a statute.

Therefore, when we consider the statutory obligations of an agent we must remember that they generally supplement common law duties, as do administrative rules. But if there is a conflict between the common law and a statute, the statute takes precedence. And administrative rules are enforceable only as long as the government agency that created them did not exceed the authority granted in the enabling statute.

Currently the License Act provides a list of obligations for a broker when representing a seller exclusively, when representing a buyer exclusively, and when operating in a dual agency. The License Act refers to these as the **affirmative obligations** of the agent. The duties when representing a seller or a buyer exclusively are –

- To exercise reasonable care and diligence
- To deal honestly and in good faith
- To present all written offers, written notices and other written communications to and from the parties in a timely manner without regard to whether the property is subject to a contract for sale or the buyer is already a party to a contract to purchase
- To disclose material facts known by the agent and not apparent or readily ascertainable to a party
- To account in a timely manner for money and property received from or on behalf of the client

- To be loyal to the client by not taking action that is adverse or detrimental to the client's interest in a transaction
- To disclose in a timely manner to the client any conflict of interest, existing or contemplated
- To advise the client to seek expert advice on matters related to the transaction that are beyond the agent's expertise
- To maintain confidential information from or about the client except under subpoena or court order, even after termination of the agency relationship
- For a seller's agent, unless agreed otherwise in writing, to make a continuous, good faith effort to find a buyer for the property, except that a seller's agent is not required to seek additional offers to purchase the property while the property is subject to a contract for sale.
- For a buyer's agent, unless agreed otherwise in writing, to make a continuous, good faith effort to find property for the buyer, except that a buyer's agent is not required to seek additional properties for the buyer while the buyer is subject to a contract for purchase or to show properties for which there is no written agreement to pay compensation to the buyer's agent.

To understand the statutory requirements for dual agency we have to start with the kinds of licenses available. Under the Real Estate License Act there are two kinds of brokers licenses – regular brokers and principal brokers. A principal broker is one who has taken additional courses and has several years of experience. To employ other brokers as subagents you must hold a principal brokers license. Either kind of broker can represent sellers exclusively, buyers exclusively, or act as dual agents.

If a broker represents both buyer and seller it is called a ***disclosed limited agency***. This could be done by a regular broker or principal broker. But sometimes you have two brokers working for the same principal broker where one represents the seller exclusively and the other represents the buyer exclusively. In this case there is a problem because the two brokers are really agents of the principal broker and the principal broker is the agent of the clients. In this case the License Act says only the principal broker is in a disclosed limited agency. The employee brokers are still an exclusive agent for the seller and an exclusive agent for the buyer.

Whenever a broker or principal broker is in a disclosed limited agency the broker owes the same duties to both parties as though it were an exclusive seller or buyer agency, plus, to both seller and buyer, (except with express written permission of the respective person), the duty not to disclose to the other person –

- That the seller will accept a price lower or terms less favorable than the listing price or terms,
- That the buyer will pay a price greater or terms more favorable than the offering price or terms, or
- Specific confidential information.

If the principal broker is the one with the disclosed limited agency then the broker representing the seller and the broker representing the buyer owe to the seller and buyer the duty to –

- To disclose a conflict of interest in writing to all parties,
- To take no action that is adverse or detrimental to either party's interest in the transaction, and
- To obey the lawful instructions of both parties.

The Real Estate License Law also modifies the common law responsibilities of the principal to third parties. At common law the principal is liable for wrongful acts of the agent as long as the agent was acting within the scope of the agent's authority. Of course, a principal would not authorize an agent to break the law, so the principal's liability is usually only for errors and omissions of the agent. Still, this could be expensive for the principal. And, while the principal has recourse against the agent to recover the loss, if the agent does not have the resources to pay the damages the principal may end up footing the whole bill.

To protect principals the License Act provides that principal is liable for the agent's wrongful acts only if the principal "participates in or authorizes the act, error or omission," and "only to the extent that the principal benefited from the act, error or omission" and even then only if it appears to a court that the claimant would be unable to enforce a judgment against the agent. (ors 696.822, for the full text, see the Appendix.) Note how this modifies the common law principle of respondeat superior.

Obligations of the principal to the agent

Of course, in an agency relationship, the agent is not the only party with responsibilities. The principal has various duties toward the agent and to third parties as well. The chief duty of the principal to the agent is to pay the compensation as agreed and in a timely fashion. If the agent has performed as agreed, and has not exceeded the authority granted by the principal or breached the agent's fiduciary obligations to the principal, then the agent is usually entitled to his or her compensation. However, it may be possible for the principal to avoid this obligation if the agent was not properly licensed at the time the agent claimed to have earned the fee, or if the agency agreement itself was not in writing or was otherwise defective.

The principal also must reimburse the agent for the agent's expenses if the agent was authorized to pay expenses in advance to others. And the principal is responsible to the agent for any losses the agent suffers as a result of the principal's wrongful acts. For example, suppose an owner gives an agent a listing agreement to sell the owner's property. The agent secures a buyer, who makes an offer, and the owner accepts. When the transaction is about to be finalized, it is discovered that there is an unrecorded lien against the property which the owner failed to disclose to the agent. The lien causes the transaction to fall through. Nevertheless, the principal must pay the commission to the agent, since the failure of the transaction was caused by the negligence of the principal, not the agent.

Obligations of the principal to third parties

The fact that the agent is required to disclose to third parties does not relieve the principal of the same obligation. In other words, if the third party is damaged, he or she has cause of action against the party or parties who caused the harm. Usually this includes the principal but it only includes the agent if, as we noted above, the agent is also negligent.

Of course, the chief obligation of the principal to third parties is to honor the actions of the agent, assuming the agent was acting within the scope of the agent's authority. Thus, if the agent was authorized to sign a rental agreement with a tenant, then the principal is bound to honor the rental agreement. The principal is also responsible to third parties for the agent's actions, even if the actions are wrongful, as long as the agent was acting within the agent's authority. The principal is not responsible to third parties for the wrongful acts of the agent if the agent acts outside of the scope of the agent's authority.

Since the agent is the representative of the principal, at common law the principal is deemed to be given notice of anything the third party communicates to the agent. This is called ***imputed notice***. In other words, if a prospective buyer wishes to put the seller on notice, the buyer does not have to tell the seller directly; telling the seller's agent

NOTES

is deemed to be the same as telling the seller. Because this provision of common law is often misunderstood by the public, the Real Estate License Act states in ORS 696.822 (3) "unless acknowledged by a principal in writing, facts known by an agent or subagent of the principal may not be imputed to the principal if the principal does not have actual knowledge," and (4) "unless acknowledged by a real estate licensee in writing, facts known by a principal or an agent of the principal may not be imputed to the licensee if the licensee does not have actual knowledge."

Exercise f

The principal must _____ the agent his or her agreed upon compensation in a timely fashion. However, if the agent had no _____ at the time the compensation was alleged to have been earned, if the agent exceeded his or her _____ or breached his or her obligations to the principal, then the principal need not pay. In addition, the agent is entitled to his or her out-of-pocket _____ which were advanced on behalf of the principal. The principal is also responsible to the agent for _____ _____ which cause damages to the agent.

The principal is also obligated to make _____ _____ to third parties, the same as the agent. The principal is not _____ for the wrongful actions of the agent, unless the principal knew of it and benefited from it. Notice to the agent is deemed to be notice to the principal; this is called _____ notice, but in Oregon the principal is deemed to have notice only if the principal _____ the notice in writing.

Seller property disclosure

Because failure to disclose material latent defects in the property has become a significant problem, the 1993 Oregon Legislature enacted a series of statutes (ORS 105.465 to 105.490 – for the full text see the Appendix) requiring sellers of residential property to complete a disclosure statement for the buyer. The form of the disclosure statement must follow the statute. A sample of the disclosure statement is reproduced on pages 69-73.

The seller disclosure requirement applies only to residential properties of one to four units which the buyer will occupy as a personal residence. Sales of brand new homes are exempt provided the builder gives the buyer a statement containing the date and jurisdiction under which the building permit was issued. Sales by financial institutions of properties acquired by foreclosure are also exempt, as are sales of properties by receivers, personal representatives, guardians, conservators and government agencies.

Even when the sale is not exempt the seller can refuse to give the buyer the completed disclosure form. If the seller gives the buyer the disclosure form the buyer has five days in which to revoke the offer to buy. If the seller refuses to give the buyer the disclosure form then the buyer can revoke the offer any time up to closing. If the buyer does nothing within the time period then the buyer's right to revoke the offer expires. Similarly, once the buyer has closed the transaction the buyer's right to re-voke expires. If the buyer revokes the offer the all deposits made by the buyer must be refunded.

Real estate agents are required to inform sellers of their obligations under the stat-ute and buyers of their right to the disclosure form.

Terminating agency relationships

General principles of contract law could create situations where an agency agreement becomes unenforceable. For ex-ample, if one of the parties enters into the agreement in reli-ance upon fraud, misrepresentation, mutual mistake of fact, undue influence, or was temporarily incompetent, then the agreement is voidable at the option of the damaged party. Similarly, if the agreement is not in writing, does not contain an adequate description of the property, or is for an illegal act, the agreement is void. Agency agreements also become unenforceable due to impossibility beyond the control of one of the parties, among many other possibilities. However, in real estate sales, agency relationships are normally ter-minated by expiration or by one of the parties unilaterally terminating it.

Notwithstanding an expiration clause, an agency contract is not necessarily ter-minated immediately when the expiration date arrives. Even though the agency contract has expired, if the principal continues to encourage the agent to work on behalf of the principal the principal will likely be held to have waived the expiration date. Even if the principal does not actively encourage the agent to continue, if the principal is aware of the agent's continuing efforts and permits the agent to proceed, the agency relationship will not be severed.

Expiration dates are also ineffective if the agent is able to rely on a safety clause in the agreement. A **safety clause** (sometimes called an **extender clause** or a **carry-over clause**) is a clause that extends an agreement for anyone the agent showed the property to during the term of the agreement. Its purpose is to prevent an unscrupulous owner from going around the agent by waiting to sell the property after the listing agreement expires. For example, suppose you have a listing agreement, which is set to expire on July 15. Shortly before the agreement expires you show the property to a prospective buyer. The owner and the buyer conspire to avoid paying your commission by waiting to execute a sale agreement until after the listing agreement expires. If you have a safety clause which lasts long enough to cover the time when the sale finally occurred, the owner still owes you the commission.

Agency agreements, the same as any agreement, can be mutually canceled or rescinded. That is, the principal and the agent can simply agree to terminate the rela-tionship. It is not uncommon in ordinary real estate practice for the principal to have a change of plans so he or she no longer wishes to sell the property. When this happens, agents try to protect themselves from an unscrupulous owner who may claim to have a change of plans, but in reality has found a buyer and wishes to sell the property without paying the commission. To keep the principal honest, most agents ask the principal, as a condition of canceling the agency agreement, to sign an agreement that if the property is sold during a period of time after the cancellation, the owner will pay the commission anyway, and if the owner enters into a new listing agreement for the property, that it will be listed with the agent.

Agency agreements fall into a special category of contracts called **personal ser-vices contracts**. There are various special rules which apply to personal services contracts. First, personal services contracts cannot be assigned, so an agent must perform the task himself or herself, although the agent may hire employees and assistants. If the principal authorizes the agent to use employees, assistants and other agents, then the principal is responsible for the employees, assistants and other agents. The agent can hire employees, assistants and other agents even if the principal does not authorize it, but then the principal is not responsible for their actions.

Another feature of personal services contracts is that they are terminated by the death, incompetence or bankruptcy of either the principal or the agent. For example, if you take a management agreement on a property and the owner dies during the term of the agency, the agency agreement is extinguished. Contrast this with an ordinary, non-agency contract, such as selling a property on a land sales contract. If either the seller or the buyer dies, the estate of the deceased person must still perform the contract. Of course, in an agency contract, if the agent dies, the agency is terminated the same as if the principal had died. This is the reason that most real estate companies (both brokerage and property management) are incorporated. If the owner gives a management agreement for the property to the corporation, the death of the broker or property manager does not terminate the agency relationship, because the broker or property manager was not the agent in the first place; the agent was the corporation.

Personal services contracts cannot be enforced by specific performance. **Specific performance** is a pleading asking a court to order a party to a contract to perform it as agreed. So if the owner wishes to withdraw the authority, or if the agent wishes to renounce the agency, neither can stop the other. However, while specific performance is not possible, a suit for damages is. So if the principal withdraws the authority wrongfully, the agent has grounds to recover damages. Note that it is not a wrongful revocation of the authority if the agent has exceeded the agent's authority or breached the fiduciary obligations to the principal.

The amount of the damages the agent is entitled to recover for a wrongful revocation depends on whether or not a transaction actually occurred. If the principal withdraws the authority and no transaction actually occurs, then the agent is entitled to recover the expenses the agent incurred up to the point of revocation. But if the principal withdraws the authority and proceeds to sell the property to someone who learned about the availability of the property during the term of the agency agreement, then the agent is generally considered to be entitled to recover the full compensation. Agents should be careful however, as this is an area of law that is not as clear in Oregon as it could be.

The rule that the principal cannot be stopped from revoking the authority has a major exception. If the agent has an interest in the property we say it is an **agency coupled with an interest**. In this case the principal may not revoke the authority without cause. For example, if the principal grants the agent a management agreement on the property, and an option to buy the property as well, then the agent has an interest in the property (the option) and the principal cannot revoke the authority. The interest can be any interest – e.g., the agent could have a leasehold, be holding a mortgage, have an easement, etc.

Agency agreements are usually **unilateral contracts**. That is, only one party can be compelled to perform; performance by the other is optional. For example, the terms of a typical listing agreement to sell a property provide that the owner promises to pay the agent if the agent secures a buyer, but the agent makes no promise that the agent will actually find a buyer – that is, performance by the agent is optional. Therefore, in most cases, the agent can renounce the agency at will, without fear of demand for damages from the principal.

However, not all agency agreements are unilateral. Suppose a broker takes a listing from a seller and guarantees that if the broker cannot sell the property the broker will buy it for a certain price (brokers commonly call this a "guaranteed sale program" and use it as a marketing tool). Notice that both parties have made promises to the other, so each has the ability to force the other to perform. This agreement is now bilateral, and the agent is not permitted to renounce the agency without being liable to the principal for damages.

Exercise 9

Agency relationships are usually terminated by _____ . *However,* _____ *of a listing or management agreement will not terminate the relationship if the* _____ *permits or encourages the agent to work on the task. In addition, a* _____ *clause in a listing provides for the payment of compensation to the agent if the* _____ *sells the property to someone the* _____ *showed the property to, even if the transaction took place after the expiration of the listing agreement. All agency agreements are contracts for* _____ _____ *so they cannot be enforced by* _____ _____ *, although performance can be compelled by a suit for damages. This also means that the* _____ *can revoke the authority at any time, but if the revocation is* _____ *, the agent may be entitled to damages. Since agency agreements are generally* _____ *, the agent can* _____ *the agency at any time, but if the agreement is* _____ *, then the agent may be liable for damages for failing to perform. However, if the agency is coupled with an* _____ *that is, if the agent has an* _____ *in the property, then the principal cannot revoke the authority. Agency relationships are also terminated by the* _____ *, incompetence or* _____ *of either principal or agent.*

Subagency

In a traditional listing or management arrangement, the owner is the principal and the broker or property manager is the agent. Typical agreements provide authority for the agent to hire the agent's own agents (**subagents**) to assist in discharging the agent's duties. Brokers may hire other licensed brokers, and licensed or unlicensed property managers as subagents. Property managers may hire other licensed or unlicensed property managers.

 **Gives listing or management agreement to** **Hires employee brokers or property managers**

Real estate subagency relationship. Subagent represents agent who, in turn, represents the owner. Thus indirectly the subagent is working for the owner the same as the agent.

NOTES

In the diagram on the preceding page, the owner is the principal, the broker or property manager is the agent, and the contract between them is a listing or management agreement. The broker or property manager, in turn, has hired a subagent. The contract between the broker or property manager and the subagent is another employment agreement. The listing or management contract between the owner and the broker or property manager probably grants numerous authorities to the agent, including the right to show the property to prospective buyers or tenants, to place a sign on the property, to advertise the property, to hire subagents, and to seek the cooperation of other brokers and property managers.

But the contract between the broker or property manager and his or her subagents contains authorities of a more general nature. Typically, it authorizes the subagents to secure new listing or management agreements for the broker or property manager, secure offers on existing properties that are available, present offers to owners and secure their acceptances, show and sell, or rent or lease, properties listed by other brokers who have requested the assistance of the broker or property manager, and the like. Normally there is also an extensive discussion of the amount of the subagent's compensation.

Subagents should take care to note that they are authorized to take listing or management agreements and other business only on behalf of the employing broker or property manager. When the subagent takes a listing or management agreement, for example, the agreement is the personal property of the broker or property manager, not of the subagent who obtained it. Therefore, if the subagent wishes to leave the broker or property manager, he or she cannot take any listing or management agreements, since they are not his or her agreements in the first place. The subagent's employment agreement may even stipulate that if the subagent leaves, he or she earns no compensation, even if the property is sold, rented or leased after the subagent leaves.

The arrangement on the preceding page with one broker or property manager and his or her subagent(s) is typical. However, many times there is another brokerage or property management firm involved. And this second brokerage or property management firm may have its own subagents, as well. In a normal, traditional transaction, this second brokerage or property management firm is also an agent of the first broker or property manager, and a subagent of the owner.

Agency arrangement with agent having employee agents and also cooperating with another real estate firm which, in turn, has its own agents as well; all representing the owner

In the scheme on the preceding page, the first brokerage or property management firm originally took the listing or management agreement, or one of the firm's brokers or property managers took it on the firm's behalf. It is the personal property of the first firm. The first firm is under no obligation to cooperate with the second firm, although if the second firm belongs to the National Association of Realtors®, their Code of Ethics may require the firm to cooperate with other members. If the first brokerage or property management firm agrees to cooperate with the second brokerage or management firm, the second firm becomes another agent of the first firm. In other words, the first firm has two agents, its own subagent, and the second firm. The contract between the first firm and the second firm is called a ***cooperation agreement***, or "coop agreement," for short.

The second firm, in turn, has hired a subagent. If the second firm's broker or property manager is the one who procured the offer from the buyer or tenant, then he or she is the subagent of the second broker or property manager (and sub-subagent, if you wish, of the first broker or property manager). Ultimately, all have a fiduciary duty to the owner.

What then of the buyer or tenant? Who is representing the third party in this typical transaction? In the majority of cases, the third party is simply without representation. Of course, a broker or property manager, either directly or via his or her subagents, may represent a buyer or a tenant instead of an owner. This is called ***buyer brokerage*** or ***tenant brokerage***. Or a broker or property manager may represent both the owner and the third party. This is called ***dual agency***. Both buyer or tenant brokerage and dual agency have their good points and their bad points, as we shall see below.

Exercise h

In traditional transactions, the owner is the _____ and the broker or property manager is his or her _____ . The typical listing or management agreement authorizes the broker or manager to hire assistants, who are the broker or property manager's _____ . The first broker or property manager usually also seeks the assistance of other brokers or property managers, who also become the owner's _____ . These brokers or property managers may also have their own _____ who are the _____ of the first broker or property manager. In this arrangement, all of the agents owe a _____ obligation to the owner.

Buyer brokerage

Buyer brokerage, as the term would imply, is when the agent represents the buyer rather than the seller. A parallel situation would exist if a broker represented a prospective tenant in a management setting. Both are not the traditional manner in which agents act.

However, representing a buyer or a tenant is a time-honored way of doing business, particularly in commercial real estate. It is not uncommon, for example, for a company to engage the services of a local real estate broker or property manager to locate property for them and to represent them in negotiations with the owner and the owner's agent. In the residential field it has become a popular alternative as well.

Single agency with buyer or tenant representation. Each principal has a separate agent

Consider the diagram above and note how it is different from the preceding diagrams. This time we have the second broker and his or her subagent representing the buyer. Although the preceding diagram, showing both brokers or property managers representing the owner, is the more common arrangement, this chart showing buyer brokerage is also common. To many real estate buyers and agents , buyer brokerage seems more logical.

In the past, buyer brokerage was used almost exclusively in commercial settings. With the rise in popularity of buyer brokerage in residential transactions, we have a solution to problems that used to occur. Suppose your sister wishes to buy a home and, quite naturally, expects you to find her one. In the past, residential agents represented only sellers. Would you seriously try to represent the seller's best interests when the buyer is your sister? Clearly, you want to advocate your sister's best interests, so buyer representation in this situation is the only practical and honest alternative.

Dual Agency

There is yet another alternative to explore. Under the law of agency, it is also possible to represent both parties. This is called ***dual agency***. However, there are some special rules for dual agency. First, there must be full disclosure to, and written permission from both parties. Considering that most brokers and property managers take listing and management agreements which only provide for ***single agency*** (representing just one side of the transaction), you would have to notify and secure written permission from each owner before showing their property.

The second problem is that all fiduciary duties are suddenly owed to both. Of course, this means that the duties must be altered. For example, you cannot have "utmost loyalty" to two different parties, so the duty becomes closer to "equal loyalty." Similarly, at common law "full disclosure" means that you cannot keep confidences from either party — whatever one party tells you must be disclosed to the other, and vice-versa. In the past, because of these problems, most agents found that dual agency was not normally the answer. Today, however, there are statutes which solve most of the problems of dual agency.

Of course, you can act as a single agent to perform certain tasks for one party, while acting as a single agent to perform other non-conflicting tasks for the other. This may appear to be a dual agency, but in reality is two separate single agencies. For example, suppose the owner gives you a listing agreement on a house, but the agreement does not authorize you to take a deposit from the buyer. (Most listing agreement forms do authorize this, but for the sake of the example, let us suppose that you have one that does not.) Now suppose you find a buyer who wishes to make an offer and also wishes to tender a $5,000 earnest money deposit. If you take the $5,000 from the buyer, you are representing the buyer, as to the act of taking the deposit, but you are still representing the best interests of the owner as to the task the owner has given you. Most agents avoid these situations. As you can imagine, making sure that the task you have accepted from one party does not conflict with your duties to the other is very difficult.

Disclosed limited agency disclosure

Today there is another issue related to dual agency. The Real Estate License Act provides for a *disclosed limited agency* and a special disclosure form when it is used (see pages 65–66). A disclosed limited agency is a special kind of dual agency used to resolve the problems involved when one agent in a company takes a listing and another agent in the same company finds the buyer.

To understand the disclosed limited agency we have to start with the kinds of licenses issued. The beginning license is called a broker's license. A broker can operate independently (called a *sole practitioner* broker) or can be affiliated with a principal broker or with other sole practitioner brokers. However, one thing a broker cannot do is supervise the professional real estate activity of other brokers. To supervise other brokers you need a principal broker's license, which requires additional education and experience. Thus, a real estate company usually has at least one principal broker.

The problem is that when a broker affiliated with a principal broker takes a listing the License Act and Administrative Rules provide that the listing belongs to the principal broker, not to the broker who took the listing. Thus, the principal broker is the seller's agent, and the broker who took the listing is the seller's subagent. Both owe common-law fiduciary duties and statutory affirmative obligations to the seller.

But now what happens when another broker affiliated with the same principal broker finds and represents the buyer? This is done with a buyer service agreement, which effectively makes the principal broker the agent of the buyer. If the principal broker is already the agent of the seller by virtue of the listing, then the principal broker is in a dual agency relationship. The License Law requires that the principal broker then give a disclosed limited agency disclosure form to the buyer and to the seller. The individal brokers are each in a single agency relationship, so they do not need to give their respective clients the disclosed limited agency disclosure form. However, as agents of the principal broker it is most likely that the individual brokers will be the ones to give the client the disclosed limited agency form on behalf of their principal broker.

In the real world of real estate practice today most principal real estate brokers simply require their affiliated brokers to give the seller the disclosed limited agency disclosure form at the time of taking the listing. Similarly, an employee broker who agrees to represent a buyer is expected to give the buyer the disclosed limited agency disclosure form at the time of entering into the buyer service agreement. If they do not then one broker affiliated with the company cannot sell a property listed by another agent in the same company without first going out to give the seller and the buyer the disclosed limited agency disclosure form.

In addition, in cases where there exists a disclosed limited agency between a principal broker and the clients, the principal broker must ensure that neither of the individual brokers have access to sensitive information. For example, the principal broker can have access to the entire transaction file, but the listing broker cannot be allowed access to the buyer service agreement and the buyer's broker cannot be allowed access to the listing agreement. As a practical matter, the principal broker generally maintains separate files for the listing and the buyer service agreements and maintains custody and control of them.

Exercise i

When a real estate agent represents a buyer, it is called _____ _____ and the agent owes a _____ obligation to the buyer. A buyer's agent may receive compensation from the _____ or from the _____ .

When a broker represents both the buyer and the seller, this is called _____ agency. In this case, the broker owes the _____ obligations as agent _____ to both parties.

Who represents whom?

As you can see, the issue of who the agent represents is far from simple. And if you think it is confusing for agents to understand, imagine how the average buyer and seller see their relationships with their agents. In fact, in residential sales, the typical buyer is frequently convinced that the agent who is showing the property is representing his or her interests and not the interests of the seller.

The confusion is made worse by the ease with which agency contracts can be created. Remember, an agency contract need not be in writing for the third party to rely on it. Nor do agency agreements require a consideration. All that is required is that the principal consent to being represented.

Consider the case of a real estate agent who has been showing property to a buyer for some time. As the agent shows property after property to the buyer, the agent is very helpful with information about the neighborhood, including recent sales prices, location of schools, and so forth. And while showing property, the agent is careful to point out latent defects, possible violations of land use laws, and other material facts which the agent wants to be sure to disclose to the buyer. When the buyer finally makes an offer, does this buyer think the agent is representing his or her best interests, or the interests of the seller?

Remember that an agency agreement can be created by estoppel. If the principal leads the agent to believe that he or she will honor an agency relationship, or if the agent acts so as to induce the principal into believing that the agent is representing him or her, an agency by estoppel may be created. In the above example, does the buyer have justification to believe that the agent was representing his or her best interests? Does "being helpful" create an agency the buyer is entitled to rely upon? If a court made such a finding, the agent would be in big trouble indeed. For if the agent were found to have been representing the buyer, after agreeing in writing to be the agent of the owner (through the listing agreement), then the agent is a dual agent. And in this case, the dual agency is undisclosed and without the consent of both parties. We refer to this kind of situation as an **unintentional** or **accidental dual agency**.

An agent of the seller may generally do any of the following for the buyer without creating an agency with the buyer:

- Give information about comparable sales in the area
- Make disclosure of material defects
- Give the buyer information and assistance with financing
- Give information about the neighborhood
- Entertain the buyer and cultivate his or her good will
- Advise the buyer to seek legal or tax counsel

The reason these are acceptable is that a selling agent's primary goal is to secure an offer for the seller. As long as the agent's actions lead in that direction, and as long as there is no direct conflict of interest, it does not matter if the actions also benefit the buyer.

However, what if the agent starts advocating the buyer's position? The agent makes statements such as "If you want to buy this property, I would start by offering $ _____ ." These are examples of actions which would justify the buyer in believing that the agent is on the buyer's side.

But what if the agent, when beginning to work with a new buyer, stated that the agent was representing the best interests of the seller? Now that the buyer has been put on legal notice of the agent's position, it will be very difficult for the buyer to claim that the agent was acting on his or her behalf.

Agency disclosure requirements

Today, the majority of states, including Oregon, require that the agent make some form of disclosure as to whom they represent. However, Oregon law requires such disclosure only in sales settings, not in property management. In the meantime, many agents who conduct property management already voluntarily disclose their position to their clients and customers.

Because of past misunderstandings of who represents whom, the Oregon Real Estate License Act requires a broker to give the prospective principal a pamphlet on agency relationships at the first contact with a buyer or seller. The pamphlet was written by the Real Estate Agency and is part of the Agency's Administrative Rules. In ordinary single agency relationships the agent is not required to give the buyer and seller a formal disclosure form (except in the case of a disclosed limited agency), although some agents do anyway. It is a good practice to give them the pamphlet and then ask them to sign a copy of the pamphlet, acknowledging receipt of it.

However, since the law does not require the agent to give a disclosure form to the principal in most cases, to ensure that the agent informed the party of which role the agent took in the transaction, the License Act provides that the sales (earnest money) agreement must contain an acknowledgment signed by the parties as to the agent's role. Thus, if the agent was acting for the seller but failed to tell the buyer that fact, the buyer would likely become angry at the time of being asked to acknowledge that the agent was acting for the seller. The law presumes that the agent would avoid this problem by making disclosure up front.

The License Act and Administrative Rules do require a formal agency disclosure if the agent will be acting in the role of disclosed limited agent. As noted previously, it happens when a principal broker in a real estate company has one employee broker representing a buyer and the buyer wants to buy a listing of one of the other brokers in the company. Remember, when the listing is taken, then the principal broker is the seller's agent. And if a broker representing a buyer works for the same real estate company, then the principal broker is the agent of the buyer as well.

Undisclosed principals

Although unusual, sometimes a buyer will ask a broker for representation and the buyer will not want the broker to disclose the buyer's identity to sellers. This usually happens in a commercial setting, perhaps where a company wishes to acquire property in an area but doesn't want it to be known that they are contemplating the move. After all, if word got out that a large company was looking for property in the area, it could increase asking prices.

When a broker works for an undisclosed principal there are some special issues to consider. Note that the usual authority of the agent in this case will be to enter into the sales contract on behalf of the principal. In the example of a large company acquiring property in the area, the seller would assume that the broker is the buyer, since the broker cannot disclose to the seller that the broker is acting as agent of the real buyer. In this case the seller can hold the real buyer to the bargain as well as the broker.

Alternatives to agency

Some real estate brokers feel that the law of agency does not fit the role they want to take in a real estate transaction. They view their job as being that of a *facilitator*, not an agent. The License Act and Administrative Rules do not specifically prohibit this. Nothing says that a real estate broker must operate under the law of agency. As noted above, the License Act and Administrative Rules do specify the duties the broker has with the seller and the buyer. But if a broker wants to be a facilitator instead of an agent, it is permitted as long as the broker follows the statutory obligations to the parties.

Nevertheless, being a facilitator is potentially more fraught with problems than being an agent. In an agency relationship the common law of agency and statutory requirements spell out exactly what the agent's duties are. If you are a facilitator you will have to create your own contract. Furthermore, over the past ten to twenty years the public has come to expect that real estate brokers are agents. People are accustomed to the relationship and deviating from it may be more trouble than it's worth.

Many years ago real estate agents were only dimly aware of the law of agency. No one ever disclosed anything to anyone. But as time went on brokers discovered that they are more respected by the public when they are open and forthright about their relationship with their clients and customers. In the final analysis, fairness and honest dealings will make for the most successful and profitable real estate practice.

KEY TERMS

The key to understanding any new field is the vocabulary used in that field. To maximize your comprehension of the material presented in this chapter, be sure you know the meaning and significance of the following terms. Remember that the majority of test questions primarily test knowledge of vocabulary.

Accidental agency

Actual authority

Actual fraud

Actual misrepresentation

Administrative rule

Affirmative obligations

Agency coupled with an interest

Agency by estoppel

Agent

Apparent authority

Attorney in fact

Authority

Buyer brokerage

Carry-over clause

Client

Commingling

Common law

Complete accounting

Confidentiality

Constructive fraud

Constructive misrepresentation

Conversion

Cooperation agreement

Customer

Disclosed limited agency

Dual agency

Due diligence

Employee

Enabling statute

Estoppel

Expressed actual authority

Expressed agency

Extender clause

Facilitator

Fiduciary

Fraud

Full disclosure

General agent

Implied authority

Imputed notice

Independent contractor

Innocent misrepresentation

Latent defect

Law of agency

Loyalty

Material fact

Negligent misrepresentation

Obedience

Ostensible authority

Personal service contract

Principal

Principal and agent

Ratification

Respondeat superior

Safety clause

Secret profit

Single agency

Sole practitioner broker

Special agent

Specific performance

Statute of Frauds

Statutory law

Straw man

Subagent

Tenant brokerage

Tort

Unfair Trade Practices Act

Unilateral contract

Unintentional dual agency

Unintentional agency

Universal agent

ANSWERS

To chapter exercises. If you couldn't figure out what to put in the blanks, find the answer here!

Exercise a

An agent is someone who represents a ___PRINCIPAL___ *. The agent has a* ___FIDUCIARY___ *duty to the* ___PRINCIPAL___ *and is generally required to have specialized knowledge. The relationship is normally created when the* ___PRINCIPAL___ *gives the agent* ___AUTHORITY___ *. Someone who signs a document for another is an* ___ATTORNEY___ ___IN___ ___FACT___ *, and is operating under a* ___POWER___ ___OF___ ___ATTORNEY___ *, a type of agency agreement. When a* ___LISTING___ *agreement is taken, the agent represents the seller. In real estate sales, it is also common today for the agent to represent the* ___BUYER___ *. Most real estate agents refer to their* ___PRINCIPAL___ *as a* ___CLIENT___ *. An agent who is given just one task is a* ___SPECIAL___ *agent. If an agent is granted authority to perform a category of tasks, the agency is* ___GENERAL___ *. When an agent has been granted unlimited authority, then we say it is a* ___UNIVERSAL___ *agency.*

Exercise b

If your income is subject to withholding taxes, then you are an ___EMPLOYEE___ *under the Internal Revenue Code. The income of* ___INDEPENDENT___ ___CONTRACTORS___ *is not subject to withholding. You are generally an* ___INDEPENDENT___ ___CONTRACTOR___ *if you and your employer follow the Safe Harbor Rules.*

Exercise c

The basis of an agency relationship is the ___AUTHORITY___ *which the principal grants to the agent. If granted orally or in writing, it is an* ___EXPRESSED___ *agency. The agency can also be* ___IMPLIED___ *, as where the agent is presumed to have certain powers. We create an agency by* ___RATIFICATION___ *when the principal grants the* ___AUTHORITY___ *after the agent has performed. Agency agreements can also be created by* ___ESTOPPEL___ *, such as in a case where one party leads another to believe there exists an agency. Then we say the authority is* ___APPARENT___ *or* ___OSTENSIBLE___ *. If the agent exceeds the agent's authority, then the* ___PRINCIPAL___ *has just cause to* ___REVOKE___ *the authority without paying the agent the* ___COMPENSATION___ *. The principal, or a damaged third party could also sue the agent for* ___DAMAGES___ *if the agent exceeds his or her authority. Exceeding your authority is also a violation of the Oregon* ___REAL___ ___ESTATE___ ___LICENSE___ ___ACT___ *, so you could also lose your license.*

Exercise d

The agent's fiduciary obligations to the principal include utmost ___LOYALTY___ *. This means that the agent must keep the best interests of the principal ahead of all others, including the interests of the* ___AGENT___ *. Also, the agent must not* ___DISCLOSE___ *confidential matters to anyone without authority from the principal. The agent owes the principal a duty of* ___FULL___ ___DISCLOSURE___ *as well. This means that a listing agent must* ___DISCLOSE___ *certain matters to the principal such as the* ___VALUE___ *of the property, the* ___FINANCIAL___ ___CONDITION___ *of the prospective buyer, any* ___RELATIONSHIPS___ *the agent has with third parties, and any other* ___MATERIAL___ *fact. The agent must also* ___OBEY___ *the principal, but not to the point of breaking the law. The agent must also give the principal a complete* ___ACCOUNTING___ *. And the agent must exercise* ___DUE___ ___DILIGENCE___ *. This means that the agent cannot accept tasks for which he or she does not have the necessary* ___SKILLS___ *, and should perform tasks as quickly and efficiently as possible. The agent's failure to honor his or her fiduciary obligations is a*

_____TORT_____ which could subject the agent to suit for _____DAMAGES_____ or loss of the agent's real estate _____LICENSE_____ . In addition the principal has just grounds to revoke the authority without being liable to the agent for the _____COMPENSATION_____ due the agent.

Exercise e

Even though the agent's _____FIDUCIARY_____ obligation is to the principal, the agent has a duty of _____FULL_____ _____DISCLOSURE_____ , honesty, good faith and competence to others. A _____FRAUD_____ is when someone makes a false statement or fails to disclose a latent _____MATERIAL_____ _____FACT_____ , yet the party knew the truth at the time. If the party was ignorant of the truth, it is a _____MISREPRESENTATION_____ . A negligent _____MISREPRESENTATION_____ occurs when the party should have verified a fact and did not. An innocent _____MISREPRESENTATION_____ occurs when the agent made a false statement but did so in reliance on a reasonable source of information. These are called _____ACTUAL_____ when the statement is made to the third party, and they are called _____CONSTRUCTIVE_____ when the party is silent, but had a duty to disclose. Failure to disclose, regardless of the level, can result in a suit for _____DAMAGES_____ or for _____RESCISSION_____ of the contract. In addition, the agent could lose his or her real estate _____LICENSE_____ if the failure to disclose was negligent or fraudulent.

Exercise f

The principal must _____PAY_____ the agent his or her agreed upon compensation in a timely fashion. However, if the agent had no _____LICENSE_____ at the time the compensation was alleged to have been earned, if the agent exceeded his or her _____AUTHORITY_____ or breached his or her obligations to the principal, then the principal need not pay. In addition, the agent is entitled to his or her out-of-pocket _____EXPENSES_____ which were advanced on behalf of the principal. The principal is also responsible to the agent for _____WRONGFUL_____ _____ACTS_____ which cause damages to the agent.

The principal is also obligated to make _____FULL_____ _____DISCLOSURE_____ to third parties, the same as the agent. The principal is not _____LIABLE_____ for the wrongful actions of the agent, unless the principal knew of it and benefited from it. Notice to the agent is deemed to be notice to the principal; this is called _____IMPUTED_____ notice, but in Oregon the principal is deemed to have notice only if the principal _____ACKNOWLEDGED_____ the notice in writing.

Exercise g

Agency relationships are usually terminated by _____EXPIRATION_____ . However, _____EXPIRATION_____ of a listing or management agreement will not terminate the relationship if the _____PRINCIPAL_____ permits or encourages the agent to work on the task. In addition, a _____SAFETY_____ clause in a listing provides for the payment of compensation to the agent if the _____PRINCIPAL_____ sells the property to someone the _____AGENT_____ showed the property to, even if the transaction took place after the expiration of the listing agreement. All agency agreements are contracts for _____PERSONAL_____ _____SERVICES_____ so they cannot be enforced by _____SPECIFIC_____ _____PERFORMANCE_____ , although performance can be compelled by a suit for damages. This also means that the _____PRINCIPAL_____ can revoke the authority at any time, but if the revocation is _____WRONGFUL_____ , the agent may be entitled to damages. Since agency agreements are generally _____UNILATERAL_____ , the agent can _____RENOUNCE_____ the agency at any time, but if the agreement is _____BILATERAL_____ , then the agent may be liable for damages for failing to perform. However, if the agency is coupled with an _____INTEREST_____ that is, if the agent has an _____INTEREST_____ in the property, then the principal cannot revoke the authority. Agency relationships are also terminated by the _____DEATH_____ , incompetence or _____BANKRUPTCY_____ of either principal or agent.

Exercise h

In traditional transactions, the owner is the _____PRINCIPAL_____ and the broker or property manager is his or her _____AGENT_____ . The typical listing or management agreement authorizes the broker or manager to hire assistants, who are the broker or property manager's _____AGENTS_____ . The first broker or property man-

ager usually also seeks the assistance of other brokers or property managers, who also become the owner's ___AGENTS___ *. These brokers or property managers may also have their own* ___AGENTS___ *who are the* ___SUBAGENTS___ *of the first broker or property manager. In this arrangement, all of the agents owe a* ___FIDUCIARY___ *obligation to the owner.*

Exercise i

When a real estate agent represents a buyer, it is called ___BUYER___ ___BROKERAGE___ *and the agent owes a* ___FIDUCIARY___ *obligation to the buyer. A buyer's agent may receive compensation from the* ___BUYER___ *or from the* ___SELLER___ *.*

When a broker represents both the buyer and the seller, this is called ___DUAL___ *agency. In this case, the broker owes the* ___FIDUCIARY___ *obligations as agent* ___EQUALLY___ *to both parties.*

PRACTICE QUESTIONS

The following practice questions are representative of the questions you will find on the final examination and on the licensing examinations given by the Oregon Real Estate Agency.

1. The law of agency concerns itself with the rights, duties and liabilities between and among
   (A) a principal and an agent.
   (B) an agent and any third party with whom the agent deals.
   (C) an agent and any third party interested in the principal's property.
   (D) all of the above.

2. Regarding powers of attorney,
   (A) anyone can hold a power of attorney.
   (B) anyone can become an attorney in fact.
   (C) both A and B are true statements.
   (D) neither A nor B is a true statement.

3. When a licensee acts on behalf of a seller, he or she is best described as
   (A) a dual agent.
   (B) an implied agent.
   (C) a fiduciary.
   (D) having a ratified agency.

4. An attorney in fact is
   I. a person acting under a power of attorney.
   II. the same as an attorney at law.
   III. someone empowered to sign another's name to a contract.
   (A) I only
   (B) I and III only
   (C) I, II and III
   (D) II only

5. Which of the following may an attorney in fact not do?
   (A) Grant a mortgage on the principal's property to a third party
   (B) Perform acts which the principal authorizes
   (C) Sell real property for the principal for compensation without a license
   (D) Sign the principal's name in the absence of the principal

6. What law prescribes the rights and duties between a property manager and the clients?
   (A) Law of agency
   (B) Statute of Frauds
   (C) Statute of Limitations
   (D) Fair Housing Act

7. The relationship between a real estate broker and the broker's principal is which of the following?
   (A) A fiduciary
   (B) An agency
   (C) Both A and B
   (D) Neither A nor B

8. A valid contract employs someone to do specific legal tasks which involve representing the interests of the principal to a third party. What kind of relationship is created by the contract?
   (A) Owelty
   (B) Lis pendens (notice of pendency)
   (C) Fee simple
   (D) Agency

9. When a broker or property manager signs a contract to manage an owner's property the licensee becomes a
   (A) lessor.
   (B) trustee.
   (C) receiver.
   (D) fiduciary.

10. John Russell, a licensed broker, was employed by Richard O'Neil to sell his home. Which of the following statements would correctly describe Russell's relationship to O'Neil?
    I. Russell is O'Neil's agent.
    II. Russell owes a fiduciary duty to O'Neil.
    III. Russell is a general agent.
    (A) I only
    (B) I and II only
    (C) II and III only
    (D) I, II and III

11. The position of trust assumed by the broker as an agent for the principal is described most accurately as a
    (A) trustee relationship.
    (B) trustor relationship.
    (C) confidential relationship.
    (D) fiduciary relationship.

12. Which of the following relationships would be fiduciary in nature?
    (A) Broker — Customer
    (B) Broker — Client
    (C) Broker — Principal broker
    (D) Both B and C

13. Which of the following are fiduciaries in a real estate transaction?
    I. Escrow agent   III. Buyer
    II. Broker   IV. Seller
    (A) I and II only   (C) III and IV only
    (B) I and III only   (D) I, II and IV only

14. An Oregon real estate broker may
    I. accept an offer which will be binding on the broker's principal, if he or she is given the proper authority by the principal.
    II. reject an offer without consulting the principal.
    (A) I only   (C) Both I and II
    (B) II only   (D) Neither I nor II

15. A a broker licensed under a principal broker is an agent of the
    (A) principal broker.   (C) fiduciary.
    (B) buyer.   (D) seller.

16. A broker took an exclusive agency listing agreement from the seller. The broker found a buyer who agreed to buy the property at the full listed price. The broker was acting as the agent of
    (A) the buyer.   (C) both A and B.
    (B) the seller.   (D) neither A nor B.

17. Which of the following situations would be a subagency?
    (A) The selling broker participates in a sale by exercising an option
    (B) The selling broker cooperates with another broker
    (C) The listing broker assigns his or her selling responsibilities to another broker
    (D) The selling principal broker assigns his or her selling responsibilities to the other brokers in the office

18. Theo Thornhump, a licensed real estate broker, was employed by a seller to sell a home. Which of the following is a correct description of Thornhump's relationship to the seller?
    I. Thornhump is the seller's agent.
    II. Thornhump owes a fiduciary duty to the seller.
    III. Thornhump is a general agent.
    (A) I only   (C) II and III only
    (B) I and II only   (D) I, II and III

19. Mr. Able hires Baker as his broker to find a buyer for his property. This creates a
    (A) special agency.   (C) universal agency.
    (B) general agency.   (D) real estate agency.

20. To the seller, a real estate broker representing the seller usually is
    (A) a general agent.   (C) an ostensible agent.
    (B) a factor agent.   (D) a special agent.

21. A licensee acting in behalf of a property owner is best described as
    (A) a dual agent.   (C) a fiduciary.
    (B) an implied agent.   (D) ratified.

22. Which of the following would be considered "dual agency"?
    I. Two brokers who are cooperating with each other to sell the same piece of property
    II. A broker who acts for both the buyer and seller
    (A) I only   (C) Both I and II
    (B) II only   (D) Neither I nor II

23. When a sole practitioner real estate broker represents more than one party to a transaction and this representation of more than one party is with the knowledge and written consent of all parties,
    i. the broker's action is called a dual agency.
    ii. the broker may legally collect a fee from only one party.
    (A) I only
    (B) II only
    (C) Both I and II
    (D) Neither I nor II

24. A real estate broker
    (A) must only act for one party in a transaction.
    (B) may act for both parties if licensed for a minimum of one year.
    (C) is a fiduciary and has the duty to remain neutral.
    (D) may act for both parties with the knowledge and written consent of both.

25. Marie Gregg acted on behalf of Tom Hilton without his authority, or even appearance of authority. At a later date, Hilton approved of her actions. Hilton's later approval of Gregg's actions would be an example of
    (A) express agreement.
    (B) ratification.
    (C) estoppel.
    (D) assumption of authority.

26. When a principal appoints someone to act on the principal's behalf, an agency relationship is created. Which of the following is not essential to establish an agency relationship?
    (A) Competency on the part of the principal
    (B) A limited power of attorney
    (C) Agreement of the parties to the agency
    (D) Capacity of the agent

27. A real estate broker generally creates his or her relationship with the client by
    (A) an expressed contract.
    (B) an implied contract.
    (C) ratification.
    (D) estoppel.

28. Broker Brown acted as agent for Mr. Smith without having authority to do so. However, Smith chose to approve of Broker Brown's unauthorized acts anyway. By doing so, Smith has created an agency by
    (A) ratification.
    (B) implied agreement.
    (C) express agreement.
    (D) estoppel.

29. Mr. Jones is led to believe by Broker Davis that Davis is Mrs. Johnson's agent, even though Broker Davis was never given the authority to represent Mrs. Johnson. From Mr. Jones' standpoint, the agency is
    (A) expressed.
    (B) actual.
    (C) ostensible.
    (D) implied.

30. On occasion, a listing agreement is said to be an "ostensible contract." In this case, we mean the contract is
    (A) one which cannot be enforced at law.
    (B) one that seems to be a contract; apparently is a valid contract.
    (C) of absolutely no legal force or effect.
    (D) voidable.

31. A seller gave a prospective buyer the impression that the broker was in fact representing the seller, even though the broker in question was never actually given any authority to represent the seller. From the buyer's standpoint, the agency was
    (A) void.
    (B) ostensible.
    (C) ratified.
    (D) voidable.

32. Tom Larsen acted on behalf of Mary Edwards without her authority, or even appearance of authority. Later, Mary Edwards approved of Larsen's activity. Her later approval of Larsen's actions is an example of
    (A) expressed agreement.
    (B) ratification.
    (C) estoppel.
    (D) assumption of authority.

33. When a principal appoints someone to act on the principal's behalf, an agency relationship is created. Which of the following is not essential to establish an agency relationship?
   (A) Competency on the part of the principal
   (B) A limited power of attorney
   (C) Agreement of the parties to the agency
   (D) Competency on the part of the agent

34. To form an agency relationship, which of the following would be the least important?
   (A) Agreement in writing
   (B) Competent parties
   (C) Consideration stated
   (D) Fiduciary relationship

35. A broker's actions with respect to a buyer can create an agency relationship even though no formal agreement was signed. Which of the following would be the most likely to result in the creation of such an agency relationship?
   (A) Showing property listed in the multiple listing service to a buyer
   (B) Presenting the buyer's offer to the seller
   (C) Negotiating price and terms with the seller on behalf of the buyer
   (D) Discussing with the buyer different financing options

36. A seller has filed a suit for damages against the broker whom the seller listed a property with, claiming that the broker really represented the buyer without disclosing that fact to the seller and obtaining the seller's permission. The buyer has testified to various statements made by the agent to the buyer. Which of the following would be most damaging to the broker?
   (A) "This property has the best view in the city."
   (B) "You should submit your offer as soon as possible."
   (C) "Let's start with an offer under the listed price."
   (D) "Let me explain about the different ways we can finance this property."

37. A real estate broker obtained a listing from the owner of property. The owner did not authorize the broker to take funds as earnest money on the property. The broker did, however, take a deposit when the broker obtained an offer from a buyer. In taking the deposit, the broker acted as
   (A) an agent of the buyer.
   (B) an agent of the seller.
   (C) an independent contractor.
   (D) a subagent of the buyer.

38. Usually, a listing contract authorizes the broker to
   I. find a buyer.
   II. bind the seller to a sales contract when a qualified buyer has been found.
   (A) I only   (C) Both I and II
   (B) II only   (D) Neither I nor II

39. In a standard listing contract, the broker acquires
   I. a fiduciary obligation toward the principal.
   II. a limited power of attorney to accept offers on behalf of the principal.
   (A) I only   (C) Both I and II
   (B) II only   (D) Neither I nor II

40. As an agent of the seller, a real estate broker is usually authorized to do all except which of the following?
   (A) Bind the principal under a sales contract
   (B) Advertise the listed property
   (C) Place a "for sale" sign on the listed property
   (D) Cooperate with other brokers to bring about a sale

41. The prime obligation of an agent to the principal is
   (A) loyalty.   (C) mutual trust.
   (B) deference.   (D) respect.

42. The position of trust assumed by the broker as an agent for the principal is described most accurately as a
   (A) trustee relationship.
   (B) trustor relationship.
   (C) confidential relationship.
   (D) fiduciary relationship.

43. Which of the following is a duty of the agent?
    (A) Completely truthful dealings with the principal
    (B) Accept only those tasks which the agent can skillfully perform
    (C) Assume full liability for any wrongful act committed or permitted by the agent or the agent's employees
    (D) All of the above

44. The property manager owes certain fiduciary duties to the principal. Which one of the following is not included in these duties?
    (A) Loyalty to the principal
    (B) Obedience to the principal's instructions
    (C) Maintenance of the property
    (D) Accountability for money and property

45. The duty of loyalty to a principal's interest requires a broker to
    I. keep the principal informed of changing market conditions.
    II. submit to the principal all written offers received on the property.
    (A) I only   (C) Both I and II
    (B) II only   (D) Neither I nor II

46. Sam is licensed under a principal broker and has taken a listing on a property. Which of the following is true?
    (A) Sam can tell a buyer how much the seller will take if the seller has already disclosed that fact to Sam.
    (B) Sam owes duties to the seller only, he owes no duties to the buyer.
    (C) Sam is the agent of the principal broker.
    (D) If Sam quits working for the principal broker, he can take his listings with him to the new broker, provided he goes to work for a new principal broker before the listings expire.

47. Broker Richard Jones knows that Donald Smith will sell his home for $15,000 less than the listed price. Broker Jones reveals this information to buyer Brown, and thereby
    (A) violates his duties as Smith's agent.
    (B) complies with the law by making full disclosure of material facts to the buyer.
    (C) offers a fraudulent inducement to buy.
    (D) performs what is known in the real estate business as puffing.

48. The broker owes the principal the duty of following the principal's instructions. In the event that the principal requires that the broker commit an unlawful act, what could the broker do?
    (A) Report the seller to the Real Estate Commissioner
    (B) Charge the seller with fraud
    (C) File a civil suit against the seller
    (D) Withdraw as the broker

49. Jim Rossiter, a real estate broker, took a listing at $285,000. He located a couple who said they would make an offer of $270,000, but stated that they would go as high as $280,000 if they had to. Jim should
    (A) buy the property for $270,000 and resell it to the buyers for $280,000.
    (B) write up and submit the $270,000 offer, but be sure to tell the seller that the buyers might go to $280,000.
    (C) try to persuade the buyers to make the $280,000 offer now.
    (D) try to persuade the buyers to make the $280,000 offer now, but if they will not, write up the offer, present it, and tell the seller that the buyers may go to $280,000.

50. A broker took a listing from a seller. The seller stipulated that the broker was not to take any type of earnest money except a cashier's check. A buyer appeared and made an offer. As earnest money, the buyer tendered a personal check for $5,000 made payable to the broker's clients' trust account. The broker should
    (A) deposit the check to the clients' trust account.
    (B) present the offer to the seller as soon as possible, and tell the seller that the earnest money is a personal check.
    (C) return the earnest money to the buyer.
    (D) do both A and B.

51. If a principal instructs the agent to make certain representations which are known to be false to both the principal and the agent, and if the agent follows those instructions, the
    I. principal is liable because he or she explicitly authorized the misrepresentation.
    II. agent will be personally liable for the misrepresentation.
    (A) I only
    (B) II only
    (C) Both I and II
    (D) Neither I nor II

52. According to the law of agency, a real estate property manager owes the principal the duty of
    I. offering legal advice.
    II. conforming with the principal's instructions.
    III. exercising reasonable care.
    (A) I and II only
    (B) I and III only
    (C) II and III only
    (D) I, II and III

53. A seller has listed property with a broker for $295,000 and instructed the broker not to present any offers under $290,000. Of the following offers, which is the listing broker obligated to present?
    (A) A full price offer, asking the seller to carry a contract for $290,000 from a buyer who the broker knows currently has six other properties, all of which are being foreclosed on
    (B) An all-cash offer of $250,000
    (C) An offer for $292,000 made through a cooperating broker, when the listing broker has a full price offer from another buyer
    (D) All of the above

54. A broker obtained a listing on a property, and the owner also granted the broker a separate option to purchase for the same term as the listing. Before the broker can exercise the option, the broker must
    (A) record a notice of intent to exercise the option.
    (B) give the seller actual notice of the broker's intent to exercise the option.
    (C) obtain the seller's written consent.
    (D) do both A and B.

55. A buyer and seller entered into an earnest money agreement through the efforts of a broker. The broker has liability to the buyer, and the buyer may have recourse against the broker, if
    (A) the broker gave the money to the seller, and the seller backed out of the transaction.
    (B) the broker acted outside the limits of the authority as granted by the seller.
    (C) the broker misrepresented facts to the buyer.
    (D) any of the above occurs.

56. When a broker accepts a note in lieu of cash as earnest money, without the knowledge and approval of the seller, and the note later cannot be collected, the seller can
    (A) declare the listing agreement void.
    (B) sue the buyer for the amount of the note.
    (C) hold the broker liable for the amount of the note.
    (D) do any of the above.

57. A buyer wishes to make an offer on a property and use a personal demand note as earnest money. Which of the following is true?
    (A) The agent can accept the note.
    (B) The agent must show on the earnest money agreement that the earnest money is in the form of a note rather than cash or a check.
    (C) The agent cannot accept a note as earnest money.
    (D) Both A and B are true.

58. After the close of a sale the seller learned that the buyer was the broker's sister. The sale was at the full listed price and terms. Which of the following is correct?
    I. The broker has violated the Real Estate License Law.
    II. The broker has violated the law of agency.
    (A) I only
    (B) II only
    (C) Both I and II
    (D) Neither I nor II

59. If an agent receives two offers at the same time before the agent has had an opportunity to present the first offer, and one of the offers is clearly better than the other, the agent should
    (A) submit both offers and let the seller decide.
    (B) make sure that both buyers know of the other's offer before presenting them.
    (C) submit the offer which the agent feels is in the best interests of the seller.
    (D) do both A and B.

60. Arnold signed a standard exclusive right to sell listing agreement appointing Steven as his agent to sell his country estate at a price of $700,000 cash. After two months, and numerous open houses, Steven obtained a cash offer from Tom for $625,000. Since Arnold was away for a week, and not wanting to lose what he now felt was an advantageous sale, Steven signed the earnest money agreement on behalf of Arnold who was shown as the principal. Subsequently, Arnold, feeling the price was too low, refused to sign the deed at closing. Based on the above facts, which of the following statements is true?
    I. Steven exceeded his authority as an agent.
    II. Tom can enforce the contract against Steven since he signed as seller.
    (A) I only
    (B) II only
    (C) Both I and II
    (D) Neither I nor II

61. A real estate broker took a listing from a seller in which the seller agreed to carry a contract with 20% down. Later, another broker appeared who had a buyer for the property. The second broker asked the listing broker to cooperate and the listing broker agreed. The second broker then secured an offer from a buyer which was at the full listed price, and the offer provided that the seller was to carry a contract with 20% down. Before this offer could be presented, the listing broker also obtained an offer from another buyer which was less than the listed price, but all cash. The listing broker should
    (A) refuse to present the second broker's offer.
    (B) present both offers, but tell the seller to accept the all-cash offer.
    (C) present both offers and let the seller decide which offer to accept.
    (D) refuse to present either offer.

62. A principal broker employed two brokers. One broker received an offer on one of the principal broker's listings. Within a few hours, the other broker obtained an offer on the same property. The brokers submitted only the first offer. In this situation,
    (A) the brokers' obligations to the seller have been violated.
    (B) the brokers have violated their obligations to their principal broker.
    (C) no violation would occur if the offers were substantially of equal merit.
    (D) both A and B are correct.

63. A broker has taken a listing on a property at a price of $339,500 and has shown it to a buyer. The buyer has made an offer of $325,000, but has indicated to the broker a willingness to go to $339,500 if necessary. The broker should tell the seller
    (A) that the buyer indicated a willingness to go to the full listed price.
    (B) that any counteroffer the seller makes voids the offer and the buyer is under no obligation to accept the counteroffer.
    (C) both A and B.
    (D) neither A nor B.

64. A broker listed a property for $250,000. The broker located a buyer who agreed to pay $250,000, but wished to offer $200,000 first to see if the seller would accept it. The owner accepted the $200,000 offer, but later learned what had happened, became angry, and refused to pay the broker's commission. In this case, the broker can recover the commission from the
(A) buyer.
(B) seller.
(C) The broker can collect a commission from either the buyer or the seller.
(D) The broker cannot collect a commission because the broker failed to disclose to the seller that the buyer would pay a higher price.

65. The broker's responsibilities in presenting to the seller a written offer to purchase include making known to the seller
    I. all written offers before the seller accepts an offer.
    II. the ramifications and practical effects of an offer.
    (A) I only
    (B) II only
    (C) Both I and II
    (D) Neither I nor II

66. When presenting an offer to a seller, the listing broker must disclose the amount of compensation the broker will be
(A) paying to a cooperating broker.
(B) paying to the broker's employee broker.
(C) receiving from the buyer for services rendered to the buyer.
(D) The broker must disclose all of the above.

67. Broker Chester Cheshire took a listing on a seller's property. Buyer Adele Adamson appeared and asked Cheshire to represent her as well. Broker Cheshire should have disclosed to the seller that he was also representing buyer Adele Adamson
(A) before commencing negotiations.
(B) at least before presenting any offers.
(C) no later than just before the seller signs the closing papers.
(D) Cheshire does not need to disclose to the seller.

68. A broker licensed under a principal broker bought a duplex in the name of a friend, and later resold it at a profit. The transaction was closed under the supervision of the principal broker, and the employee broker provided that the principal broker received the usual principal broker's share of the commission at closing. Later, the seller learned that the buyer was a straw man for the employee broker. In this case
(A) the employee broker might lose his or her license.
(B) the principal broker might be responsible to the seller for the profit the employee broker made on the deal.
(C) the employee broker might be responsible to the principal broker and to the seller for the amount of the profit on the deal.
(D) all of the above are possible.

69. When a broker does not obey the principal,
(A) the broker must bear any losses.
(B) the principal must bear any losses.
(C) the broker and the principal can be held jointly and severally liable for any losses.
(D) neither party can be held responsible for any losses.

70. Since Broker Jim Jones knows that Joe Smith will sell his home for $25,000 less than the listed price, he reveals this information to prospective Buyer Ed Brown and thereby
(A) violates his duties as Smith's agent.
(B) complies with the law by making full disclosure of material facts to Brown.
(C) offers a fraudulent inducement to buy.
(D) performs what is known in the real estate business as puffing.

71. Larry Loophole, a real estate broker, took a listing on Mr. Jones' house for $300,000, which was market value. The seller wanted a fast sale, so the seller told Larry he would take as little as $250,000 if necessary. Larry located a buyer and suggested that the buyer offer $250,000. The buyer made the offer of $250,000 and the seller accepted it. Which of the following statements is true?
    (A) Larry Loophole was unethical, but did not violate any laws.
    (B) Larry Loophole violated his fiduciary obligations to the seller.
    (C) Larry Loophole violated his fiduciary obligations to the buyer.
    (D) Both B and C are true.

72. A real estate agent representing the seller should inform the client about the potential for financial damages from taking a large
    I. purchase money note.
    II. earnest money deposit.
    (A) I only
    (B) II only
    (C) Both I and II
    (D) Neither I nor II

73. Which of the following is a duty of the agent?
    (A) Completely truthful dealings with the principal
    (B) Accept only those tasks which the agent can skillfully perform
    (C) Assume liability for wrongful acts committed or permitted by the agent or the agent's subagents
    (D) All of the above

74. A broker acting as a property manager of a building was instructed by the owner to paint the building for $5,000. Without the owner's knowledge and consent
    I. the broker could contract the job for $4,000 and keep the extra $1,000.
    II. the broker could accept a rebate from the painter.
    (A) I only
    (B) II only
    (C) Both I and II
    (D) Neither I nor II

75. If legal problems arise in a real estate transaction, the broker should
    (A) recommend an attorney the broker thinks would be good.
    (B) engage an attorney to solve the problems and give advice.
    (C) notify the parties involved that they should obtain a competent attorney.
    (D) call the title company involved and request that they send an attorney.

76. A buyer asked the listing broker if it would be possible to move in prior to closing. In this kind of situation, the broker should
    (A) obtain the owner's written consent before granting permission to the buyer.
    (B) require the buyer to sign a rental agreement.
    (C) refuse to grant permission to the buyer.
    (D) do both A and B.

77. In the event a broker violates his or her fiduciary obligations to the principal, the principal can
    (A) sue for damages.
    (B) terminate the agency relationship.
    (C) refuse to pay the agreed upon compensation.
    (D) do all of the above.

78. A property manager, acting as an agent,
    I. owes care, loyalty, obedience, accounting, and notice to the principal.
    II. must maintain the owner's funds in a bank clients' trust account.
    (A) I only
    (B) II only
    (C) Both I and II
    (D) Neither I nor II

79. A seller instructed the broker not to disclose to buyers that there are structural defects in the property. The broker should
    (A) inform buyers of the defect only if the buyers specifically ask about the structure.
    (B) put the phrase "as is" into the earnest money agreement.
    (C) say nothing to the buyers because doing so would exceed the authority granted by the principal.
    (D) inform all buyers of the condition of the structure.

80. A seller of a parcel of real property told the broker that the roof leaked in the house on the property and a statement to that effect was included in the listing agreement. The seller told the broker to inform all prospective buyers of this fact, but the broker sold the property and failed to tell the buyer that the roof leaked. What recourse does the seller have against the broker if the buyer sues the seller for misrepresentation? The seller

    (A) can recover damages from the broker.
    (B) cannot recover damages because the principal is solely liable for the acts of the agent.
    (C) must seek redress only with the Real Estate Agency.
    (D) has no recourse because of caveat emptor.

81. Broker Abel took a listing on Baker's house and sold it to Charlie. Shortly after closing, Charlie discovered that the electrical wiring was defective. Baker told Abel of the problem, but Abel failed to tell Charlie. In this situation, Charlie can

    (A) collect damages from Abel.
    (B) collect damages from Baker.
    (C) collect damages from both, jointly and severally.
    (D) sue Baker, who in turn, has a claim against Abel.

82. Jones owned an apartment building and wished to sell it. Smith was a real estate broker who knew that Jones wished to sell, although Jones never gave Smith a listing on the property. Smith negotiated with Edwards in an attempt to get Edwards to make an offer. Jones was aware of these negotiations and allowed Smith to continue. Edwards finally made an offer, which Jones accepted. If Jones made any misrepresentations to Edwards during the negotiations, Edwards has a right to rely on the representations because

    (A) Smith's agency is expressed.
    (B) Smith is Jones' general agent.
    (C) Smith has an ostensible agency created by estoppel.
    (D) buyers may always rely on representations of licensees.

83. A seller listed a property for sale with a real estate broker. However, the seller failed to tell the broker about the defective chimney. The chimney defect was hidden from view. Unaware of the problem, the broker failed to tell the buyer of the defect. After closing, the buyer discovered the defect. The buyer can take legal action against

    (A) both the seller and the broker.
    (B) the broker only, since it was the broker who failed to disclose the defect.
    (C) the seller only, since it was the seller's fault that the defect was not disclosed.
    (D) no one, since the buyer has a duty to inspect the property.

84. Mr. Orland Brown was the owner of a single-family residence. He engaged his son in law, who was not licensed as an electrician, to do electrical work in preparing the home for sale. Mr. Brown did not disclose this to Broker Baker at the time of signing the listing. After the sale was completed, the new owner suffered financial losses due to the faulty electrical wiring done by Orland Brown's son in law. Broker Baker

    (A) could be severely reprimanded for not warning the purchaser prior to his executing the earnest money offer.
    (B) is innocent of any wrongful act.
    (C) could be held liable for the monetary damages suffered by the owner.
    (D) was in violation of the Real Estate License Law.

85. Owner Alpha owned a house and hired her daughter to do plumbing work on the premises, even though the daughter was not a licensed plumber. Alpha listed the property with broker Baker, but did not disclose that the plumbing had been installed by an unlicensed person. Baker then sold the property. After the buyer closed the sale the buyer suffered losses as a result of faulty plumbing installed by the seller's daughter. Broker Baker

    (A) could suffer disciplinary action by the Real Estate Agency for failing to disclose the defects to the buyer.
    (B) could be held liable for damages by the buyer.
    (C) could be held liable for damages by the seller.
    (D) has done nothing wrong.

THE LAW OF AGENCY – PRACTICE QUESTIONS

86. Mr. and Mrs. Brown listed their home with broker Bennett. At the time of the listing, the Browns withheld from Bennett the fact that there was dry rot in the structure. When Bennett secured an offer from Mr. and Mrs. Adams, they continued to withhold the information about the dry rot from Bennett and the buyers, although they accepted the Adams' offer. Shortly thereafter, Mr. and Mrs. Adams rescinded the contract when they discovered the dry rot. Broker Bennett is entitled to
(A) the full commission.
(B) one-half the regular commission.
(C) out-of-pocket expenses.
(D) the full commission plus punitive damages.

87. A seller told the broker that the walls were fully insulated at the time the seller listed the property with the broker. This information was stated in writing in the listing agreement. The buyer asked about insulation and the broker quoted the seller's statement. After closing, the buyer discovered that there was no insulation in the walls. In this case, the buyer can recover from
(A) the seller.
(B) the broker.
(C) both the seller and the broker, although the seller will have recourse against the broker for any losses.
(D) no one, as the buyer has a duty to inspect.

88. The seller told the broker that termites have destroyed the floor and that the swimming pool is in violation of the city setback requirements. Which of the following must the broker's agent disclose to a prospective buyer?
I. The condition of the floor
II. The pool violation
(A) I only
(B) II only
(C) Both I and II
(D) Neither I nor II

89. It is wrong for a broker representing the owner to
(A) tell a buyer that a house has a leak in the roof.
(B) reveal that a house has drainage problems during the winter.
(C) confide to a buyer that a home owner will take less than the list price.
(D) None of the above are improper.

90. Broker Jonas Whale took a listing from a seller of a split level home. While showing the property to a buyer, the seller pointed out to the buyer that the home could easily be converted to a duplex, since the downstairs family room with fireplace could be used as a living room and there was already a bath and bedroom in the downstairs. On the way back to the office, the broker told the buyer that the seller was probably not aware that the property was not properly zoned for a duplex. By telling this to the buyer, the broker was
(A) violating his fiduciary obligations to the seller.
(B) subjecting himself to disciplinary action for violation of the Real Estate License Law.
(C) Both A and B are true.
(D) Neither A nor B is true.

91. A broker listed the seller's house and subsequently sold it to a buyer. At the time of the listing, the seller mentioned to the broker that the water heater leaked, but that it did not matter since the property was vacant and the water was turned off. The broker never mentioned this to the buyer. After the buyer moved into the property and discovered the defect, the buyer sued the broker and the seller. Which of the following is the most likely result of the suit?
(A) The seller will be held solely responsible.
(B) The broker will be held solely responsible.
(C) The broker and the seller will both be held responsible, but the seller will have recourse to the broker for any losses.
(D) The buyer will probably lose the suit, since the buyer should have inspected the property.

92. A seller listed a home with a broker. At the time the broker took the listing, the broker asked if the property was connected to a sewer, and the seller affirmed in writing that it was. Later the broker learned that the property was not, in fact, connected to the sewer. Subsequently, the broker located a buyer who purchased the property. During the sale, the buyer did not ask and the broker did not volunteer the fact that the property was not connected to the sewer. After moving in, the buyer discovered the truth and became angry. In this case, which of the following is true?
    (A) The broker is liable to the buyer for any loss.
    (B) The seller is liable to the buyer for any loss.
    (C) The buyer had a duty to investigate, since whether or not a property is connected to a sewer is a matter of public record.
    (D) Both A and B are true.

93. A buyer made a thorough visual inspection of a property and agreed to purchase it "as is." After closing, the buyer discovered that the furnace, which appeared to be sound on the outside, was really hopelessly defective and unrepairable on the inside. The buyer can
    (A) recover nothing.
    (B) recover the cost of repair or replacement of the furnace from the broker if the broker knew of the defect.
    (C) recover the cost of repair or replacement of the furnace from the seller if the seller knew of the defect.
    (D) do both B and C.

94. Constance Trueheart purchased a property from Shifting Sands Realty, an assumed business name of the broker. After moving in, Constance discovered a material defect in the property. She complained to the broker, who disavowed any responsibility, because it was an oral listing which is not enforceable under the Statute of Frauds. In this case, the broker is
    (A) not liable.
    (B) liable, because a broker is responsible for any actions while appearing to act as an agent, even if not an agent.
    (C) not liable, because only a principal can be held liable for latent defects.
    (D) not liable because of the Real Estate License Law.

95. A broker took an offer and a deposit from a buyer, presented the offer to the seller, and the seller accepted the offer. The broker deposited the earnest money into the broker's clients trust account. If the seller later cannot deliver marketable title, what should the broker do with the earnest money deposit?
    (A) Return it to the buyer
    (B) Spend it on the seller's legal expenses in attempting to obtain good title
    (C) Retain it the same as a forfeited earnest money deposit
    (D) Leave it in the clients trust account pending the outcome of any legal disputes between the seller and the buyer

96. A real estate broker may lose the right to a commission in a real estate transaction if
    I. guilty of a misstatement of known material facts.
    II. not licensed when hired as an agent.
    (A) I only   (C) Both I and II
    (B) II only   (D) Neither I nor II

97. Dennis and Susan Miller withheld some material information from both their broker, Robert Fisher, and the buyers, Rita and Melvin Canfield, in selling a parcel of real property. Fisher obtained from the Canfields an earnest money agreement at the full listing price. Sometime after the Millers signed the agreement, the Canfield's negated the contract because of the withheld information. Fisher is entitled to
    (A) a full commission.
    (B) compensation through court action.
    (C) out-of-pocket expenses.
    (D) half of the usual commission plus out-of-pocket expenses.

98. A broker has earned the commission, even if the
    I. otherwise qualified buyer decides, for good reason, not to buy.
    II. buyer cannot obtain the financing specified in the earnest money agreement.
    (A) I only   (C) Both I and II
    (B) II only   (D) Neither I nor II

99. An earnest money receipt was signed by both the buyer, Laura Jones, and the sellers, Jack and Amy Robinson. But the transaction fell through because Amy Robinson refused to sign the deed conveying title. The broker handling the transaction
   (A) is entitled to a full commission.
   (B) is entitled to half of the commission specified in the listing agreement.
   (C) must transfer the earnest money from the clients' trust account to a neutral escrow agent on the broker's own initiative.
   (D) has violated the broker's fiduciary obligation to Jones.

100. In order for a broker to recover a commission on an open listing, the broker must prove
   (A) that the broker is duly licensed.
   (B) that the broker found a ready, willing and able buyer.
   (C) that the broker was the procuring cause.
   (D) all of the above.

101. A real estate broker working for a principal broker who has not received a lawfully earned commission may sue
   (A) the seller.
   (B) the principal broker.
   (C) both A and B.
   (D) neither A nor B.

102. If a broker wishes to receive a commission from both a buyer and a seller, the broker must have
   (A) listing agreements from both parties.
   (B) the knowledge and consent of both.
   (C) permission from the Real Estate Agency.
   (D) both A and B.

103. A broker took a listing on a property for $300,000 and secured a full price offer from a buyer. The seller accepted the buyer's offer. The broker placed the earnest money, in the amount of $15,000 in the broker's clients' trust account. However, before closing, the buyer and seller mutually agreed to rescind the transaction and the seller instructed the broker to return the buyer's earnest money. In this situation, the broker should
   (A) inform the seller that the $15,000 was being retained as part of the commission and demand that the seller pay the rest of the commission directly.
   (B) refund to the buyer only that portion that the "forfeited earnest money" clause in the listing or earnest money agreement calls for, and keep the residue as part of the commission.
   (C) retain the $15,000 in the broker's clients' trust account until the broker can renegotiate a new sales agreement between the buyer and seller.
   (D) refund the $15,000 to the buyer and make demand on the seller for the full commission.

104. A broker sold a large parcel of land as the owner's agent. The broker may accept the commission in the form of
   (A) cash from the sales proceeds.
   (B) a note from the buyer.
   (C) a note from the seller.
   (D) any of the above.

105. When notice is given to an agent, to the principal this notice may be called
   (A) unintentional notice.
   (B) constructive notice.
   (C) imputed notice.
   (D) either B or C.

106. Which of the following will terminate an agency relationship created to sell real property?
   I. Bankruptcy of either principal or agent
   II. Change of business address of either principal or agent
   III. Death of either principal or agent
   IV. Destruction of the property
   (A) I and II only   (C) II and III only
   (B) I and III only   (D) I, III and IV only

107. An owner of property gave a listing to a broker. Shortly thereafter the owner died. In this case the
   (A) agency is immediately terminated.
   (B) broker is entitled to the full commission from the estate.
   (C) listing agreement is binding on the heirs of the deceased owner.
   (D) broker is entitled to a reasonable time thereafter to procure a buyer during which time the listing will remain in force.

108. Vera Riche listed her property with a broker. Soon thereafter, she died. In this case, the
   (A) agency is immediately terminated.
   (B) broker is entitled to the full commission from the estate.
   (C) listing agreement is binding on the heirs of the owner.
   (D) broker is entitled to a reasonable time after the owner's death to procure a buyer, during which time the listing remains in force.

109. A woman who owns an apartment building hired an agent to collect the rent. As of the first of the month, the agent had collected all of the rents, save one. On the second of the month, the owner died. The following day the agent attempted to collect the rent from the late tenant, whereupon the late tenant refused to pay the rent to the agent. The tenant's refusal to pay the rent to the agent was
   (A) legal, because the agency was terminated.
   (B) illegal, because a contract entered into while alive is binding on the decedent's estate.
   (C) illegal, because the estate has the inherent right to collect the rent.
   (D) illegal, due to the specific provisions of the Oregon Residential Landlord and Tenant Act.

110. An owner of a property gave a listing on it to a broker. Shortly thereafter, the owner died, even though most of the term of the listing still remained. In this case,
   (A) if the broker brought about a sale during the remaining term of the listing, the broker would be entitled to the full commission from the estate.
   (B) the listing agreement would be binding upon the heirs of the deceased owner.
   (C) the agency would be immediately terminated.
   (D) the broker would be entitled to a reasonable time after the owner's death in which to secure an offer on the property.

111. Property manager Jack Benson's property management agreement with Larry Graham may be terminated by
   I. destruction of Graham's rental property.
   II. mutual consent.
   III. expiration of the agreement.
   (A) III only   (C) II and III only
   (B) I and II only   (D) I, II and III

112. Ben Hogan listed his property with Broker Sam Fastpen. Shortly thereafter, with time remaining on the listing, Hogan died. The listing
   (A) terminated at Hogan's death.
   (B) is binding on Hogan's heirs.
   (C) will continue in force until the normal agreed expiration date arrives.
   (D) must be reaffirmed by the personal representative of Hogan's estate.

113. Abrahams gave a 90-day listing to Broker Samuels. One month later, Abrahams died. Samuels, unaware of Abrahams' death, obtained an offer for the property from Thomas. Concerning Thomas' offer, which of the following is correct?
   (A) Abrahams' estate must sell the property to Thomas and pay a commission to Samuels.
   (B) Abrahams' estate does not have to sell the property to Thomas, but does owe Samuels a commission.
   (C) Abrahams' estate must sell the property to Thomas, only if Thomas agrees to pay the commission.
   (D) Abrahams' estate is not required to sell the property or pay a commission.

114. Broker Adams, a sole proprietor, took a six-month listing on a property, which was subsequently placed in the multiple listing service. Five days after the property was listed, Adams died. Ten days after Adams' death, a cooperating broker secured an offer on the property. Which of the following is true?
(A) Adams' wife could assume the listing and present the offer to the seller.
(B) If the seller accepts the offer, a commission is due to Adams' estate.
(C) The listing agreement terminated at Adams' death.
(D) Any commission due on the sale would be payable to Adams' heirs.

115. Ted Logan signed a property management agreement with property manager John Burton for a 90-day period. Shortly thereafter Logan died. The agreement
(A) terminated at Logan's death.
(B) is binding on Logan's heirs.
(C) will continue to be valid until the 90-day period expires.
(D) must be reaffirmed by the personal representative of Logan's estate.

116. Which of the following would terminate a listing agreement?
I. Destruction of the property
II. Full performance by the broker
III. Mutual agreement to cancel
IV. Expiration of the listing period.
(A) I, II, III and IV   (C) III only
(B) II and III only   (D) III and IV only

117. A broker took a listing on a property. Later the seller was disabled and confined to a wheelchair. In this case, the
(A) agency was terminated by the disability of the principal.
(B) broker must obtain a power of attorney from the principal.
(C) agency relationship was voidable at the option of the principal.
(D) agency was unchanged.

118. A seller listed property with a real estate broker. Which of the following events would not terminate the agency relationship?
(A) The marriage of the seller
(B) Bankruptcy of the seller
(C) Revocation of the authority prior to the expiration of the listing
(D) Withdrawal from the agency by the agent

119. Samuel Adams listed his house for sale with the real estate firm of Dilley, Dalley, Doolittle and Stall for 180 days. After 90 days the property had not yet sold, and Adams changed his mind about selling. Adams then instructed the firm to take the property off the market. The agency relationship is terminated
(A) on the 180th day of the listing.
(B) when the firm receives the instructions to take the property off the market.
(C) as soon as Adams relists the property with another broker.
(D) on the earlier date of A or C.

120. An agency coupled with an interest means
(A) the broker has made a secret profit at the expense of the broker's principal.
(B) the broker received an interest-bearing note in payment of the broker's commission.
(C) a suit has been filed for commission and the broker filed a lien on the seller's property.
(D) the agency cannot be terminated by the principal before the expiration date.

121. A seller cannot terminate a broker's listing agreement if the
(A) broker has made attempts to negotiate a sale.
(B) broker has advertised the property.
(C) broker holds an interest in the property.
(D) owner desires to change brokers.

122. A broker is acting as agent for a buyer. The broker's fee can be paid by
(A) the buyer.   (C) the listing broker.
(B) the seller.   (D) any of the above.

123. In respect to realtionships of real estate agents, a broker
    (A) who is representing the seller exclusively is not permitted to act on behalf of anyone whose interests are at variance with the interests of the principal.
    (B) must make full disclosure to the buyer of every material latent defect the broker knows about the property.
    (C) Both A and B are true.
    (D) Neither A nor B is true.

124. In Oregon, a broker may
    (A) not cloud the title to a property by recording a claim for a commission.
    (B) take a net listing on a property.
    (C) collect a commission from both parties to a transaction, if both parties know of the commission from the other and give their consent.
    (D) All of the above are true.

125. If a legal question were to arise as to whether a broker was a buyer's agent or not, which of the following would be significant?
    (A) Which party or parties paid the broker
    (B) Whether there was a listing contract
    (C) Whether the buyer asked the broker for assistance in locating a property
    (D) All of the above

126. A real estate broker
    (A) must act for only one party in a transaction.
    (B) may act for both parties after one year of license experience.
    (C) is a fiduciary, and therefore must remain neutral.
    (D) may act for both parties with the knowledge and written consent of both.

127. A broker may engage in an undisclosed dual agency in
    (A) residential transactions.
    (B) commercial transactions.
    (C) sales of real estate securities.
    (D) no case.

128. Bonnie is a broker affiliated with a principal broker. She has taken a listing and now wishes to buy the property. She intends to collect the normal share of the commission as the listing broker and as the selling broker, since she is, in effect, "selling" it to herself. In this situation, she represents
    (A) the seller.
    (B) the buyer.
    (C) both the buyer and the seller as a dual agent.
    (D) neither the buyer nor the seller.

129. When there is an exchange transaction, the broker usually owes a fiduciary obligation to
    (A) the first party to contact the broker only.
    (B) the buyer only, since the first buyer is also a seller.
    (C) both parties, since each performs as both seller and buyer.
    (D) neither, since their interests conflict.

130. Barry Beanhead, a broker working for himself as a sole practitioner, took a listing on a property. Later he located a buyer who wished to enter into an exchange agreement with the seller for some other property the buyer owned. Barry took a listing on the buyer's property and then prepared an exchange offer to present to the first client. In this case, Barry is most likely acting as agent for
    (A) the first client only.
    (B) the second client only.
    (C) both the first and the second client in a disclosed limited agency.
    (D) neither party.

131. When can the broker accept compensation from both the buyer and the seller?
    (A) The broker may never accept compensation from both buyer and seller.
    (B) The broker may accept compensation from both buyer and seller if both have given the broker a listing.
    (C) The broker may accept compensation from both the buyer and the seller if disclosure is made to both and both consent.
    (D) Both B and C are required before a broker may accept compensation from both the buyer and the seller.

132. A broker listed a house for $175,000 and sold it for full price on FHA terms. The buyer gave the broker a note for $5,000 as earnest money. The broker then certified to a lending institution that there is earnest money in the amount of $5,000 in the broker's clients' trust account. In this case
     (A) the broker has committed a fraud on the lender.
     (B) the Real Estate Agency could revoke the broker's license.
     (C) both A and B are possible.
     (D) neither A nor B is possible.

133. The amount of commission a principal broker must pay a broker from a real estate sales transaction is determined by
     (A) the listing agreement.
     (B) local agreement of brokers.
     (C) mutual agreement between the principal broker and the broker.
     (D) the earnest money agreement.

ANSWERS

To practice questions. If you chose the wrong letter, here's the right one! The explanations are designed to clarify your understanding.

1. **D** Not only does the law of agency concern the relationship between a broker and the broker's principal, but also the relationship(s) between the agent and third parties, such as the other party to the transaction, lenders, appraisers, and anyone else involved in the transaction.

2. **D** A power of attorney is created when someone (a principal) grants authority to another to perform a certain task, or tasks, for the principal. These tasks typically take the form of signing documents on behalf of the principal. The person hired is an agent. When acting under a power of attorney, the agent is called an attorney in fact. Since the attorney in fact is acting on behalf of the principal, he or she must have the same capacity as the principal, i.e., he or she must be of legal age, mentally competent, and so forth. Therefore "anyone can hold a power of attorney" is not a true statement.

3. **C** All agents are fiduciaries of their principals. The broker is a fiduciary to both the principal broker under whom the broker is licensed and to the owner. It is also possible to be a dual agent, to create an implied agency or to create the agency by ratification, but these are unusual in normal real estate practice.

4. **B** An attorney in fact is someone acting under the authority of a power of attorney. An attorney in fact need not be licensed to practice law, but must be competent. You become an attorney in fact under a power of attorney.

5. **C** Assuming the principal granted the necessary authority, the attorney in fact may act as the principal's agent to perform all of the listed tasks. However, selling the property for compensation requires a license as well as authority.

6. **A** A property manager acts under the law of agency, the same as a real estate broker. Only the tasks are different; the legal obligations of the parties to each other are the same.

7. **C** In a real estate listing, the seller is the principal and the broker is the agent. The agent owes a fiduciary duty to the principal, which includes the duty of loyalty, obedience, full disclosure, complete accounting and due diligence.

8. **D** When a parcel was owned by co-tenants and was partitioned, sometimes the size of the partitions will not equal the original interests. If one party pays something to the other to equalize the division, the money paid is called owelty. A contract to represent another is an agency contract, governed by the law of agency. Fee simple is a type of real estate ownership. A lis pendens is a cloud on an owner's title.

9. **D** When you become an agent, you are granted authority by the principal, and you also have obligations to the principal. The obligations of the agent to the principal are called the fiduciary obligations.

10. **B** An agency agreement is created when an agent agrees to represent a principal. The agent has a fiduciary duty to the principal, which includes the duty of loyalty, obedience, full disclosure, complete accounting and due diligence. A special agent is one who is given one task to perform. A general agent is given multiple tasks, typically a category of tasks. A universal agent is empowered to do anything on behalf of the principal. When a real estate agent takes a listing, he or she is given one task.

11. **D** An agency agreement is created when a principal agrees to be represented by an agent. The agent owes a fiduciary duty to the principal, which includes the duty of loyalty, obedience, full disclosure, complete accounting and due diligence. A trustor is one who gives something to a trustee, with instructions to hold it for the benefit of a third party, the beneficiary. The trustee is a fiduciary, but not generally an agent.

12. **D** An agent always has a fiduciary obligation to the principal. Principals are frequently referred to by agents as their clients, but third parties to whom no fiduciary obligation is owed are called customers. Not only does the broker owe a fiduciary duty to the principal (client), but the broker's licensee is also the broker's agent and owes the same duty to the broker as the broker owes the principal. In other words, in a typical real estate transaction, the principal broker is at the same time the agent of the owner, and the principal to the brokers associated with the principal broker.

13.   **A**   When a principal hires an agent to perform some task for the principal, an agency contract is created. The agent then owes duties as a fiduciary to the principal. There are many such agency contracts in real estate. A broker representing the seller is one, as is an escrow agent (closing agent) to both the buyer and the seller. Note that the buyer and seller would always be principals.

14.   **A**   The agent's authority can include the ability to do any task(s) the principal wishes to authorize. However, even if a principal authorizes a broker to reject certain offers, the agent must disclose to the principal that the offer(s) exist and are being rejected. This is because one of the fiduciary obligations of the agent to the principal is full disclosure.

15.   **A**   The License Act provides that a broker can be licensed as a sole practitioner or under a principal broker. The broker is, therefore, the agent of the principal broker. The principal broker, in turn, is the agent of the seller (under a listing) or of the buyer (under a buyer's service agreement). Although you cannot say the broker is the buyer's or seller's agent, it would not be incorrect to refer to the broker as the subagent of the buyer or seller.

16.   **B**   How much the buyer offers and what kind of listing the broker has are irrelevant. Any listing makes the broker the agent of the seller. Unless the broker formally renounces the agency with the seller, the broker is still the agent of the seller.

17.   **B**   A subagency exists when the agent hired and authorized by the principal hires his or her own agents to assist in performing the task given by the principal. The agent's relationship with the principal is a personal services contract, and so it cannot be assigned. However, subagents and assistants can be hired. When a listing broker cooperates with another broker, the second (selling) broker is presumed to become the listing broker's agent, and seller's subagent unless the selling agent has a pre-existing buyer's service agreement.

18.   **B**   A special agent is an agent who is given one specific task or authority to perform. A general agent is an agent who is authorized to perform various tasks, usually a category of tasks. A universal agent is granted unlimited authority, such as a conservator, guardian, or one who is operating under a universal power of attorney.

19.   **A**   Normally, a listing grants the agent authority for one task, so the agent is a special agent. A general agent is an agent who is authorized to perform various tasks, usually a category of tasks. A universal agent is granted unlimited authority, such as a conservator, guardian, or one who is operating under an ulimited power of attorney.

20.   **D**   There are three levels of agency. A special agent is one who is given one task to perform. A general agent is given multiple tasks, typically a category of tasks. A universal agent is empowered to do anything on behalf of the principal. When a real estate agent takes a listing, he or she is given one task, so it is a special agency. An ostensible agency is a term used to describe an agency that was not created by an expressed agreement. It is either implied or created by estoppel. There is no such thing as a factor agent.

21.   **C**   If an agent acts for just one side of a transaction, then it is called a single agency. It is possible to act for both parties, in which case it is called a dual agency. If the licensee is acting for the property owner, then he or she is acting for just one side, so it is not a dual agency. An implied agency is where the authority was not stated, but implied from good custom. The term "ratified," in contract law, merely means "agreed upon after the task was performed." All agents owe a fiduciary duty to their principals and can be called fiduciaries.

22.   **B**   Under the law of agency, an agent may work for one party or the other party (either of which is referred to as "single agency"), or the agent can act for both parties ("dual agency"). When two brokers work together to sell the same piece of property, it is conceivable that it could be a dual agency, but unlikely. Normally, one broker is the listing broker, and therefore has a single agency with the seller. The other broker either acts as a single agent for the buyer, or acts as agent of the listing broker. In either event, both brokers have single agencies, as they are representing only one party. It is a dual agency only when a broker represents both sides of a transaction.

23.   **A**   Under the law of agency, an agent may work for one party or the other party (either of which is referred to as "single agency"), or the agent can act for both parties ("dual agency"). The agent owes a fiduciary duty to the party he or she represents. Regardless of which party the agent represents, the agent can collect compensation from either one, or both, provided full disclosure is made. The fact that a broker collected compensation from a party does not necessarily mean that the broker is representing that party.

24.   **D**   There are three ways an agent can act. An agent can be a single agent representing just an owner, or a single agent representing a buyer or tenant, or the agent can be a dual agent and represent both. In a dual agency relationship, the fiduciary duties become owed to both, although certain adjustments become necessary. For example, loyalty becomes "equal loyalty," "complete accounting" is owed to both, etc.

25.   **B**   An agency relationship is created when a principal grants authority to an agent. Agents must take care not to exceed their authority, as doing so would make them liable to the principal and to third parties for damages. However, in contract law, the term "ratification" means agreeing to the contract after it was performed. It could be argued that the ratification is a form of agreement, and since it was expressed, it was an expressed agreement, but "ratification" is the obvious answer. Estoppel means that someone has been barred from asserting a right. Assumption of authority is what the agent did before the wrongful act was ratified.

26.   **B**   An agency agreement is created when a principal consents to representation by an agent. General principles of contracts apply to the agency agreement – that is, it cannot be entered into under duress, there must be a legal object, there must be a meeting of the minds, etc. There is a special issue in agency contracts regarding competence. Normally, the parties need to have been competent only when they entered into the contract. Contracts are normally still enforceable, even if one party becomes incompetent later, (although a conservator may have to be appointed by the court). However, an agency contract does become unenforceable by a future incompetence of either party. While a power of attorney is a type of agency, there are other types of agency agreements as well.

27.   **A**   Agency relationships in real estate are normally expressed. This occurs when a principal formally grants authority to the agent, such as when a seller lists a property or an owner enters into a property management agreement with a broker. Buyer's service agreements are also expressed agency agreements. An agency is also created when a principal broker and a broker enter into a formal employment agreement where the broker is to act on behalf of the principal broker.

28.   **A**   Agency relationships in real estate are normally expressed, but they can also be created by ratification. Ratification occurs when the principal agrees to the authority after the agent has performed the tasks. Once ratified the agency is just as enforceable as if it had been created before the agent performed the task.

29.   **C**   When someone leads another to believe an agency exists, then it will generally exist, even though not formally expressed. Such agencies are said to be created by estoppel, that is, the party who led the other to rely on the agency is estopped (barred) from denying the existence of the agency. They are also referred to as apparent or ostensible, since they exist because the authority "appears" to exist.

30.   **B**   "Ostensible" is a synonym for "apparent," that is, a contract which appears to be a contract. Agency relationships are sometimes created when one party leads the other to believe that the agency exists, even though no formal contract was signed.

31.   **B**   An ostensible contract is a contract which a court upholds because it appears there is a contract, even though the parties may never have entered into a formal agreement. This happens when one party leads the other to believe that the contract exists. If the broker or the seller act as though the broker is representing the seller, the buyer may gain the right to assume that the relationship does exist.

32.   **B**   Agencies can be created by expressed agreement, by ratification or by estoppel. Ratification of the agency means that the agent performed the task or acted on behalf of the principal, originally without authority, but the principal authorized the acts later. Ratification makes the contract fully enforceable.

33.   **B**   Under the equal dignities rule of law, an agent cannot have the authority to do anything that the principal did not have the legal right to do himself or herself. Therefore, the agent must be competent, and the principal must be continually competent to grant the continuing authority to the agent. A limited power of attorney is only one agency among many possible kinds of agencies.

34.   **C**   Since agency relationships are consensual and not strictly contractual, a consideration is not required. Although not all agency relationships need be in writing, most real estate agency relationships must, so the consideration is the least likely to be required.

35.   **C**   Showing property to a buyer, presenting the buyer's offer, and discussing financing options with the buyer are not necessarily inconsistent with representing the seller. Therefore, the agent can do

all of these without becoming the buyer's agent. But if the agent negotiates "on behalf of the buyer" the agent has taken a position advocating the buyer's interests and this may create an ostensible agency by estoppel. Since the license law requires the agent to give an informational pamphlet to the customer at the beginning of the relationship, such misunderstandings are less common today.

36. **C** Of the choices, only suggesting that the buyer start by offering under the listed price is inconsistent with representing the seller, so this is the only answer which could result in an agency by estoppel.

37. **A** Most listing forms authorize the broker to secure an earnest money deposit from the buyer. If the listing says nothing, the agent must have received authority from someone, so if the authority did not come from the seller, it must have been implied from the buyer. Note that the broker can be an agent to both, without being a dual agent, as long as the authorities do not create a conflict.

38. **A** The amount of authority the principal gives the agent can range from one single task, to unlimited authority. In a listing agreement, the broker typically takes the authority to show and advertise the property, place it in the multiple listing service, and secure offers. The broker can, but usually does not take the authority to accept an offer on behalf of the owner. In property management agreements, the agent does take the authority to enter into contracts on behalf of the owner; i.e., the manager agrees to rent the property and sign the rental agreements on behalf of the owner.

39. **A** A listing makes the broker the agent of the seller. All agents owe a fiduciary obligation to their principals. It is possible for an agent to take the authority, whether in the listing or in a separate document, to perform any legal task on behalf of the principal, including accepting an offer. In fact, in property management, this is commonly the way agents operate – the agent accepts the authority to enter into rental agreements with tenants. But standard listing agreements do not contain the authority for the broker to accept an offer to buy on behalf of the seller.

40. **A** The key to understanding the agency relationship is that the principal gives authority to the agent. The amount of authority the principal gives the agent can range from one single task, to unlimited authority. In a listing agreement the broker typically takes the authority to show and

advertise the property, place it in the multiple listing service, and secure offers. The broker can, but usually does not take the authority to accept an offer on behalf of the owner. Note that, if the agency agreement does not specifically grant the authority, the agent does not have the authority. I.e., if a listing is silent about whether the broker can place a sign on the property, the broker cannot place the sign.

41. **A** The agent owes a fiduciary duty to the principal, which includes the duty of loyalty, obedience, full disclosure, complete accounting and due diligence. In some texts, "loyalty" is stated as "utmost loyalty." Loyalty could even be said to encompass the other fiduciary obligations. Notwithstanding the fiduciary obligations of the agent to the principal, there is no legal obligation that the parties respect each other, trust each other, or show deference to each other.

42. **D** When principal hires an agent to perform some task for the principal, an agency contract is created. The agent then owes duties as a fiduciary to the principal. Confidentiality is one of the duties, but the word "fiduciary" is the word which describes the relationship. A trustor-trustee relationship is also a fiduciary relationship, but brokers do not normally act as trustees for their clients.

43. **D** An agent owes fiduciary duties to the principal. These include loyalty, full disclosure of all facts pertinent to the agency, obedience (but not to the point of breaking the law), a complete accounting for all funds and property coming into the agent's possession on behalf of the principal, confidentiality, and due diligence. Due diligence includes accepting only tasks which the agent can perform and, once the task has been accepted, perform it in a legal manner acceptable to the principal. Everyone is liable for his or her wrongful acts and the wrongful acts of his or her employees.

44. **C** The agent owes a fiduciary duty to the principal, which includes the duty of loyalty, obedience, full disclosure, complete accounting and due diligence. While a typical management agreement will require the manager to take charge of maintenance, this is by contract and not inherent in the agency relationship. It is possible to take a management agreement without agreeing to be responsible for maintenance; it is not possible to be an agent without being responsible for loyalty, obedience, and a complete accounting.

45.   **C**   The agent owes a fiduciary duty to the principal, which includes the duty of loyalty, obedience, full disclosure, complete accounting and due diligence. Full disclosure means disclosure of any material fact pertinent to the agency. This would include all written offers. If the agent has a replationship with the third party, this would be material to the interests of the principal and must also be disclosed.

46.   **C**   The fiduciary obligations to the principal include loyalty, full disclosure, obedience, a complete accounting and due diligence. These duties include the agent's obligation to maintain confidential those communications from the principal which are privileged. However, the agent and the subagents do owe the buyer the responsibility of full disclosure of material latent defects and fair and honest dealing. Since the broker in this case is the agent of his principal broker, the broker has taken the listings for the principal broker; they are the principal broker's personal property. Therefore the broker has no right to take them with him if he leaves the principal broker's employment.

47.   **A**   The agent has an obligation to make full disclosure of material latent defects in the property, but at the same time maintain confidential those communications from the principal which are privileged. Puffing includes sales talk which is not necessarily strictly true, but which were not meant to be taken literally, such as "this is the best buy for the money."

48.   **D**   The agent owes a fiduciary duty to the principal, which includes the duty of loyalty, obedience, full disclosure, complete accounting and due diligence. However, the duty of obedience does not extend to breaking the law. As a technicality, the agent does not have to withdraw from the agency; the agent can simply refuse to commit the unlawful act. However, in this question, none of the other choices are correct.

49.   **D**   The broker who has taken a listing has a fiduciary obligation to obtain the highest price and the best terms from the buyer. The broker also has a duty of full disclosure to the broker's principal. The broker in this question may also have a problem with accidental dual agency, since the buyer apparently believes that the broker is representing the best interests of the buyer.

50.   **D**   The fact that a principal has given instructions to an agent does not affect the buyer; i.e., the buyer is not a party to the agency agreement between the seller and the broker. Therefore, the buyer is free to make whatever offer the buyer wishes. The broker must disclose everything to the broker's principal (the seller in this case), so the offer must be presented. If earnest money is received, the Real Estate License Law generally requires that it be deposited to a clients' trust account, although it can also be deposited to a neutral escrow depository if the broker has the written permission of all parties with an interest in the funds.

51.   **C**   An agent owes fiduciary duties to the principal. These include obedience (but not to the point of breaking the law), among other duties. If the principal insists that the agent break the law, the agent can either ignore the illegal instructions, or withdraw from the agency. If the agent breaks the law, the agent is liable, just as if the agent had done so without the instructions of the principal. The principal will also be liable to the third party.

52.   **C**   An agent owes fiduciary duties to the principal. These include loyalty, full disclosure of all facts pertinent to the agency, obedience (but not to the point of breaking the law), a complete accounting for all funds and property coming into the agents possession on behalf of the principal, confidentiality, and due diligence. Due diligence includes accepting only tasks which the agent can perform and, once the task has been accepted, perform it in a legal manner acceptable to the principal. Assuming the agent is not an attorney, then the agent does not have the duty to offer legal advice. Note that the agent may have the duty to advise the principal to seek legal advice, however.

53.   **D**   Part of the fiduciary obligations of the agent to the principal is full disclosure. This includes the obligation to present all offers regardless of what they are or who obtained them.

54.   **C**   When the broker takes a listing, the broker assumes a fiduciary obligation of loyalty, full disclosure, obedience, complete accounting and due diligence to the principal. If the broker also takes an option to purchase the property himself or herself, then the broker has a conflict of interest. This conflict must be resolved lest the principal have the right to claim that the broker did not exercise loyalty and due diligence.

55.   **D**   In a real estate listing, the seller is the principal and the broker is the agent. The agent owes a fiduciary duty to the principal. The agent's duty to third parties is generally limited to full disclosure,

competence, and fair and honest dealings. Full disclosure includes only those matters which are material and latent, and which the broker knew about, could have known about, or should have known about. Failing to disclose, or misstating information about material, latent defects is misrepresentation or fraud, and the agent would be liable to the buyer for damages. The agent must also act within the scope of the authority granted by the principal. If the third party is damaged as a result of the agent exceeding his or her authority, then the agent is liable to the third party. When a buyer gives money to an agent, even if the agent is acting on behalf of a seller, the agent has a duty to the buyer to return the money if it turns out that the buyer is entitled to a refund. In the above example, if the seller refuses to return the money to the buyer, the buyer has recourse against the broker.

56. **D** Part of the broker's fiduciary obligations to the seller is the duty of full disclosure. If the broker violates this duty the principal is entitled to recover from the broker any damages the broker caused; in this case, the amount of the uncollectible note. Violation of any fiduciary obligation is also grounds for revocation of the authority, so the seller can declare the listing agreement void. And, of course, the note is payable to the seller, so the seller has every right to enforce collection by suit against the buyer.

57. **D** Notes are commonly used as earnest money. The law of agency requires the agent to make full disclosure to the principal of all matters pertinent to the agency. Since there is a possibility that the note may be uncollectible, the seller must be told that the earnest money is in the form of a note.

58. **C** Any violation of the law of agency by a real estate licensee is also a violation of the Real Estate License Law. The broker has a duty to disclose any material fact to the broker's principal. If the broker fails to disclose, but there results a sale at the listed price, the seller will have no cause of action for damages, but it is still a violation of the broker's fiduciary obligation to the broker's principal which could result in loss of the compensation and disciplinary action against the broker's license.

59. **D** The fiduciary obligation of full disclosure requires that both offers be presented. The agent should also tell each buyer of the offer from the other, not out of duty to the buyers, but because doing so may result in one or both of the buyers raising their offer(s). The agent is not required to tell the buyers

how much the other offer is; but only of the existence of the other offer.

60. **A** An agency relationship is created when a principal grants authority to an agent. There are many different kinds of agencies, so the exact authority varies considerably. In most agency relationships, the principal grants to the agent the authority to enter into some kind of contract with third parties, as where an insurance company allows its agents to bind temporary insurance contracts with customers. In real estate, property managers usually take the authority to enter into rental and lease agreements with tenants on behalf of the owner. In sales, however, while possible, it would be highly unusual for an agent to take the authority to accept an offer on behalf of the seller. Assuming this was a standard listing agreement, by accepting the offer on behalf of the owner, the agent exceeded his authority. When an agent exceeds his or her authority, the agent is liable for damages to both the principal and the third party.

61. **C** The broker owes the principal the duty of full disclosure, which includes the duty to present all offers, regardless of whether they are good or not. The broker's fiduciary obligation to the principal includes the obligation to make recommendations based on the broker's experience and knowledge of the marketplace, but the final decision rests with the seller.

62. **D** The brokers are agents of the principal broker and subagents of the seller, so they owed their principal broker a duty of full disclosure, a duty which they failed to discharge. The principal broker is the seller's agent and owes the seller a duty of full disclosure, which the principal broker failed to do. The principal broker is responsible for the actions of the principal broker's employee brokers. Even if the offers were equal, both must be presented to the seller because the brokers' fiduciary obligation to the seller includes full disclosure.

63. **C** A broker with a listing is the agent of the seller, and therefore owes the duty of full disclosure, utmost loyalty and due diligence. It is true that a counteroffer will normally extinguish the offer, and the broker's duty of full disclosure includes the duty to be sure that the seller is aware of that fact.

64. **D** Full disclosure includes disclosure that the buyer will pay more when the agent is representing the seller. Since the broker violated the broker's fiduciary obligations to the principal, the broker loses the right to collect the agreed compensation and may be liable to the principal for damages as well.

65. **C** An agent owes fiduciary duties to the principal. These include full disclosure of all facts pertinent to the agency, among other duties. Full disclosure includes presenting all offers, disclosure of relationships with third parties, disclosure of the third party's financial abilities, and any other facts pertinent to the agency. Disclosing the ramifications and practical effects of an offer is also a duty, although the duty stops short of giving legal advice.

66. **C** The agent must disclose to the principal all material facts. How much the broker pays the broker's employe brokers and other subagents is not material to the seller, unless it changes the amount the seller is obligated to pay the broker, which it normally would not. However, if the broker receives compensation from the buyer, this could affect the broker's position and recommendation regarding the offer, so the listing broker must disclose that fact to the seller.

67. **B** The seller is the broker's principal, and is entitled to full disclosure of facts which are material to the seller's interests. As long as disclosure of the relationship with the buyer is made before the seller accepts an offer from the buyer, the seller's interests have not been compromised.

68. **D** Using a straw man to create a secret profit is a failure of full disclosure to the principal. This makes the agent liable to the principal for any losses suffered by the principal. The agent also loses the right to collect the agreed compensation. It is also a violation of the Real Estate License Law. The fact that the principal broker did not necessarily know of the employee broker's wrongful act does not excuse the principal broker from liability, since the principal broker is responsible for the actions of the principal broker's agents.

69. **A** Assuming there are losses from the broker's failure to obey the principal, which is a duty the broker has toward the principal, the principal will be the one who suffers the loss. Since the broker was the cause of the loss, the principal has cause of action against the broker to recover the damages.

70. **A** The question assumes that Broker Jones was acting as a seller's agent (had a listing). An agent always owes to the principal the duties of loyalty, full disclosure of facts pertinent to the agency, a complete accounting, due diligence and confidentiality. To the other party, the agent owes the duty of full disclosure and fair and honest dealings. While it would appear that the agent owes full disclosure to both sides, the matters which must be disclosed are different. In

this case, to the buyer the broker owes the duty to disclose material latent defects in the property or violations of land use laws, but not the duty to disclose privileged communications from the principal. To the seller (the broker's principal) the broker owes a great deal more.

71. **B** Although a listing broker owes a duty of full disclosure to both seller and buyer, the duty to the buyer is only of material latent defects. The agent is required to maintain loyalty to the principal, including keeping privileged information confidential.

72. **A** Purchase money note refers to the note for which a mortgage or trust deed is the lien instrument. In other words, if a seller is taking a purchase money note, the seller is carrying the financing. If the loan amount is close to the value of the property, this could be dangerous for the seller. A large earnest money deposit, however, creates greater assurance to the seller that the buyer will perform.

73. **D** The agent's duties to the principal include loyalty, full disclosure of material facts, obedience, complete accounting for all funds and property coming into the agents possession on behalf of the principal, accept responsibilities for the agent's own actions and the actions of the agent's employees and agents, and due diligence.

74. **D** This is a secret profit, and not only violates an agent's duty of full disclosure, but also subjects a real estate licensee to disciplinary action.

75. **C** The agent owes a fiduciary duty to the principal, which includes the duty of loyalty, obedience, full disclosure, complete accounting and due diligence. However, these duties do not include the giving of legal advice, which the agent is prohibited from doing. It is permissible for the agent to engage an attorney to represent the clients, but unlikely the agent would want to do so. Title insurance companies have attorneys to represent their best interests, not the interests of buyers and sellers. The normal practice is for the agent to advise the client to seek the advice of an attorney of the client's choosing.

76. **D** The key here is the extent of the authority the seller granted to the agent. If it was a normal listing agreement, it did not include the authority to enter into contracts on behalf of the principal, not even rental agreements, so the agent must have the principal sign the rental agreement or obtain permission from the principal to sign it on behalf of the principal. Agents must take all contracts in writing because to do less would not be exercising reasonable care and skill.

77. **D** If the agent violates the agent's fiduciary obligations to the principal, the usual penalty is that the principal can revoke the authority (cancel the agency agreement). The principal can also refuse to pay the agent the agreed upon compensation. And the principal may sue the agent for any damages the agent caused to the principal.

78. **C** When you become an agent, you are granted authority by the principal, and you also have obligations to the principal. The obligations of the agent to the principal are called the fiduciary obligations and include loyalty, full disclosure, a complete accounting, obedience, confidentiality, and due diligence. The Real Estate License Law requires that all licensees maintain all funds not yet belonging to the licensee in a clients' trust account.

79. **D** While a broker owes a fiduciary obligation of obedience to the principal, nevertheless the broker cannot break the law. The law requires the seller, and therefore the seller's agent as well, to disclose material latent defects in the property. These defects must be disclosed, even if the buyers do not specifically ask. Clauses in a sales contract stipulating that the buyers take the property "as is," "in its present condition," and the like, are effective only as to those defects of which the buyer was aware.

80. **A** The law requires the seller to disclose to the buyer all material, latent defects that the seller knew about, or that the seller could have or should have known about. If the broker was aware of the problem, then the duty extends to the broker as well. The principle of caveat emptor (let the buyer beware) is of little legal effect today.

81. **C** The principal is not liable for the acts of the principal's agent, including wrongful acts, unless the principal participates in or authorizes the act, error or omission. Of course, the broker is responsible for his or her own wrongful actions.

82. **C** It does not matter how the agency was created. As long as it exists, the agent's duties toward the agent's principal and third parties are the same.

83. **C** In most states, the broker cannot be held responsible for the wrongful actions of the principal. Unless the broker had some way of knowing about the defect, the broker's misrepresentation (failure to disclosse) is innocent. However, the seller's failure to disclose is either fraud or negligent misrepresentation, and the buyer can recover damages from the seller.

84. **B** The agent's duty to third parties is generally limited to full disclosure, competence, and fair and honest dealings. Full disclosure includes only those matters which are material and latent, and which the broker knew about, could have known about, or should have known about. "Material" means that the buyer would have offered less money, different terms, or not have offered to buy at all if he or she had known the truth. "Latent" means hidden from view. In this example, the defect was material and was latent, but the broker did not know, and had no reasonable way to know, about the defect.

85. **D** In this situation, the broker's failure to disclose was innocent and the buyer has no cause of action against the broker. This assumes the faulty plumbing was not visible and there was nothing to make the broker suspicious. The seller, of course is guilty of fraud or misrepresentation and the buyer has cause to sue the seller for damages.

86. **A** The broker has been damaged because the broker sold the property in good faith, but since there was no closing, the broker has not collected the commission the broker rightfully earned. The seller is responsible for the broker's loss. Therefore, the broker is entitled to recover the commission from the seller.

87. **A** In most states, the broker will not be held liable, unless there was some reason to suspect the truth of the seller's statements. In any event, even if the broker is held liable to the buyer, the broker has recourse against the seller for the misrepresentation the seller made to the broker which was the primary cause of the loss.

88. **C** The law requires the seller to disclose to the buyer all material, latent defects that the seller knew about, or that the seller could have or should have known about. If the broker was aware of the problem, then the duty extends to the broker as well. The principle of caveat emptor (let the buyer beware) is of little legal effect today.

89. **C** One of the fiduciary obligations of a broker to the principal is confidentiality, so a broker representing the seller cannot disclose to the buyer a privileged communication from the seller, such as the fact that the seller will accept less than the listed price. However, the duty of confidentiality to the seller does not extend to concealing material latent defects in the property from the buyer. The seller, and the seller's agent, must disclose to a buyer all material, latent defects that they knew, that they could have known, and that they should have know about the property.

90. **D** The broker would be guilty of violating the broker's fiduciary obligations to the seller and would be subjecting himself or herself to disciplinary action by the Real Estate Agency if the broker failed to disclose to the buyer that the seller's statements were false. This is because an agent of the seller must nevertheless disclose to a buyer all material latent defects in the property that the agent knows about, or could have or should have known about.

91. **C** The seller must disclose to the buyer any material latent defects in the property. If the water is turned off, a leak in the water heater would be considered latent. The broker owes the same duty to the buyer for material latent facts that the broker knew about. Since the seller told the broker about the defect and the broker failed to pass the information on to the buyer, the broker is the cause of any losses and is liable to the buyer for damages. The principal is not liable for the acts of the principal's agent, including wrongful acts, unless the principal participates in or authorizes the act, error or omission. In this case the principal was as much a party to the fraud as the broker.

92. **D** In this case, the broker is at fault because the broker knew of the problem. In other words, even if the seller fails to disclose to the broker, the broker has a duty to disclose to the buyer if the broker discovers the problem through the broker's own efforts. The seller is probably also liable to the buyer because, although the seller may not have known, it is something that the seller could have and should have known.

93. **D** The faulty furnace is a latent defect which is a material fact and must be disclosed to the buyer. The buyer can recover from the seller and/or the broker, depending on which was at fault for failure to disclose. Clauses in a sales contract stipulating that the buyers take the property "as is," "in its present condition," and the like are effective only as to those defects of which the buyer was aware.

94. **B** The seller and the seller's agent owe a duty of full disclosure of all material latent defects in the property. If the broker is the seller's agent, then the broker is responsible, along with the seller, for the failure to disclose. Since the broker acted as the seller's agent, an agency by estoppel has been created which the buyer has a right to rely on.

95. **A** While the broker owes a fiduciary duty to the seller, the broker has an obligation to the buyer of honesty, fair dealing and full disclosure of latent defects. Since the broker took the buyer's deposit, if the

buyer ends up entitled to a refund, the broker is liable to the buyer for the refund.

96. **C** The agent owes a fiduciary duty to the principal, which includes the duty of loyalty, obedience, full disclosure, complete accounting and due diligence. If the agent violates the fiduciary obligations to the principal, the principal has various remedies. The principal could sue the agent for damages, the principal has the right to terminate the agency agreement, and the principal does not have to pay the agent. In addition, the Real Estate License Act requires that an agent must have been licensed at the time the compensation was earned (ORS 696.710).

97. **A** The principal owes a duty of full disclosure and to pay the agent's compensation as agreed. A selling broker normally does not get paid if the broker does not do what he or she was hired to do – produce a buyer who is ready, willing and able. But if the buyer is ready, willing and able, and the transaction fails because of the wrongful actions of the principal, the agent is still entitled to the compensation.

98. **D** The agent is entitled to be paid if the agent has done what he or she was hired to do. This means that the agent may sometimes be entitled to payment, even if the transaction does not close. For example, if the seller refuses to sell, even after accepting the buyer's offer, the agent is still entitled to be paid. However, if the agent does not perform according to the terms of the agency agreement, then the agent is not entitled to be paid. A seller's agent is generally required to produce a buyer who is ready, willing, and able to buy. "Ready and willing" mean the buyer signs the papers and closes. "Able" means the buyer could command the cash or credit to close.

99. **A** A broker is entitled to be paid when the broker has performed the task for which he or she was hired. A listing generally requires that the broker produce a buyer who is ready, willing and able. If the buyer is ready, willing and able, but the transaction fails to close because of the seller's wrongful actions, the broker is still entitled to be paid. When a broker takes a listing from a seller, the broker is normally representing just the seller; not the buyer. The broker's owes fiduciary obligations to the seller only, not to the buyer.

100. **D** The agent is entitled to be paid if the agent has done what he or she was hired to do. This means that the agent may sometimes be entitled to payment, even if the transaction does not close. For example,

if the seller refuses to sell, even after accepting the buyer's offer, the agent is still entitled to be paid. However, if the agent does not perform according to the terms of the agency agreement, then the agent is not entitled to be paid. A seller's agent is generally required to produce a buyer who is ready, willing, and able to buy. "Ready and willing" mean the buyer signs the papers and closes. "Able" means the buyer could command the cash or credit to close. In open and exclusive agency listings, the broker must also demonstrate that the agent was the procuring cause of the sale. Demonstrating that the agent was the procuring cause is not required if the listing is an exclusive right to sell listing.

101.　**B**　The principal broker is the seller's agent. The employee broker is the agent of the principal broker. The listing is the personal property of the principal broker, not of the employee broker. Therefore, the employee broker has no contract with the seller, and cannot sue to collect. However, the employee broker does have a contract with the principal broker, and is entitled to whatever remedies the employee broker's employment agreement with the principal broker calls for.

102.　**B**　It is not necessary to be someone's agent in order to collect compensation from the person. However, if you collect compensation from someone whose interests are opposed to the interests of your principal, you owe your principal a duty of full disclosure. And you also owe full disclosure to the person who is paying you as to whether you are acting still as a single agent for your principal, or as a dual agent for both. In neither case is there a requirement that you involve the Real Estate Agency.

103.　**D**　If the buyer and seller mutually agree to rescind, then all parties must be placed in the same position they were in before they entered into the contract, as far as is practical. This means every party to the transaction must give everything back. But since the broker did what the broker was hired to do (secure an acceptable offer from a buyer), and has not given the seller just cause to refuse to pay, the broker is entitled to the compensation.

104.　**D**　A principal and the agent can agree on any type of compensation, including no compensation, since an agency relationship need not be supported by consideration to be enforceable.

105.　**C**　At common law the agent is acting in the place of the principal. Therefore, not only is everything the agent says the same as the principal saying it, but everything that is said to the agent is deemed to have been said to the principal as well. Thus, anything the buyer says to a seller's agent is considered notice to the seller. Another expression for this type of notice is imputed notice. However, ORS 696.822 (3) states "unless acknowledged by a principal in writing, facts known by an agent or subagent of the principal may not be imputed to the principal if the principal does not have actual knowledge."

106.　**D**　Federal bankruptcy laws, in order to give the referee or trustee in bankruptcy a free hand with the assets of the bankrupt, provide that any agency agreement to sell an asset of the bankrupt is terminated when the bankruptcy is filed. Any contract is terminated when the subject of the property is destroyed by an act of God. Death or future incompetence do not terminate ordinary contracts. However they do terminate contracts for services, including, of course, agency agreements. Unless there is a contract provision providing for termination if one of the parties should change location, a change of business address would have no effect on an agency contract.

107.　**A**　Death or future incompetence do not terminate ordinary contracts. However they do terminate contracts for services, including, of course, agency agreements. The broker would be entitled to the full commission from the estate, but only if the broker had already sold the property before the owner's death. Since the question did not say the property had been sold, we have to assume that the broker had not sold it.

108.　**A**　Agency relationships are terminated by the death, or of the future incompetence of either principal or agent or by bankruptcy of the principal. The termination is absolute except that if a transaction was entered into while the agency was still valid, the agent has a reasonable time to close it.

109.　**A**　Death of either principal or agent terminates an agency. The Oregon Residential Landlord and Tenant Act does provide that the tenant must pay the rent in good faith. But the tenant has no obligation to pay it to the former agent.

110.　**C**　Death of either the principal or the agent terminates the agency. The agent has a reasonable period of time in which to conclude any transactions entered into during the agency, but new business cannot be conducted.

111.　**D**　Agency agreements become unenforceable by the same circumstances that would render any contract unenforceable – lack of a legal object, lack of a meeting of the minds, destruction of the premises, fraud, incompetence, etc. However, agency agreements are contracts for services, which make them subject to special rules. For example, contracts for services, need not be supported by consideration. Also, contracts for services cannot be enforced by specific performance; a suit for damages is the sole remedy. And unlike most contracts, agency contracts are terminated by future incompetence or death of either party. Bankruptcy also terminates an agency agreement.

112.   **A**   Death of either the principal or the agent terminates an agency relationship. The listing can be reaffirmed by the personal representative of the deceased owner's estate, but there is no requirement that the personal representative relist the property with the original agent.

113.   **D**   Death of either the principal or the agent terminates an agency. But if the estate knew the broker was continuing to work on a sale and did nothing to dissuade the broker from doing so, then a commission would be due the broker when the broker brings about a sale, since an agency by estoppel would be created. In this case the estate has no obligation to accept the offer or to recognize the existence of the agency agreement.

114.   **C**   Death of either the principal or the agent terminates an agency relationship. Agency agreements are contracts for services, and therefore cannot be assigned and cannot be assumed by another. If the seller's estate accepts the offer it still owes no commission because the agency was terminated.

115.   **A**   Death or future incompetence do not terminate ordinary contracts. However they do terminate contracts for services, including, of course, agency agreements.

116.   **A**   Agency agreements can be mutually rescinded or canceled, can have an expiration date (real estate listings must always have an expiration date), and like all contracts, are considered canceled after full performance.

117.   **D**   Death or incompetence of either the principal or the agent terminates an agency relationship. However, physical disability is not incompetence, therefore, the agency relationship is not terminated or changed in any way.

118.   **A**   The principal can always revoke the authority, thus canceling the agency relationship. If this is done without just cause, the agent is entitled to damages from the principal, but the agency is

still terminated. The agent can renounce the agency (withdraw) also, and since most agency relationships are unilateral agreements, the seller is usually powerless to prevent it. Bankruptcy of the seller will also terminate an agency relationship. But if either party becomes married, the agency relationship is unaffected, since marriage does not create any property rights in Oregon.

119.   **B**   The principal can always revoke the authority, thus canceling the agency relationship. If this is done without just cause, the agent is entitled to damages from the principal.

120.   **D**   An agency coupled with an interest means that the agent has an interest in the property beyond merely having a listing on it. For example, a seller gives a broker a listing on the property, and also an option to buy it. Because revoking the authority created by the agency contract could adversely impact the agent's other interest in the property, the rule is that the agency cannot be withdrawn if it is an agency coupled with an interest.

121.   **C**   The fact that the broker has commenced the task of selling the property only means that the seller will owe the broker damages if the seller wrongfully withdraws the authority. The seller can still revoke the authority. However, the principal's right to revoke the authority is ineffective if the agent has an interest in the property.

122.   **D**   An agent represents the principal with whom the agent has established an agency relationship. This relationship stands whether there is compensation to the agent or not, since agency relationships do not require a consideration to be enforceable. In addition, the agent can receive compensation from others as well. However, if the agent receives compensation from the principal's adversary, e.g., the agent represents the seller, but accepts compensation from the buyer, then the agent must disclose this fact to the principal.

123.   **C**   A dual agency is legal provided the agent makes full disclosure and obtains the consent of both parties. An agent is acting in place of the principal, so if the principal is a seller, the agent must disclose to a buyer everything that the seller would have to disclose, including material latent defects.

124.   **D**   If a broker clouds the principal's title in an effort to force the principal to pay what the broker feels the principal owes to the broker, even if the broker's claim is valid, the broker will have harmed the principal for the broker's own gain, thereby violating the broker's fiduciary obligations to the

principal. A net listing is a listing where the seller is to net a certain minimum amount, and the agent's commission is to be everything the property sells for above the amount the seller is to net. Net listings are illegal in many states and unethical under the National Association of Realtors® Code of Ethics, but are legal in Oregon. Dual agencies are permitted in Oregon, provided the broker has the knowledge and prior consent of both parties. And the License Act provides that the fact that one party or the other paid the commission is "not determinative" of whom the broker was representing.

125. **D** If the broker has a listing on the property this would create a presumption that the broker was a seller's agent. However, one of the broker's employee brokers could subsequently enter into a buyer agency agreement with a buyer. If a buyer asks for any kind of assistance and the broker provides the assistance, this could be construed as working on behalf of the buyer, thus establishing a buyer agency by estoppel. The License Act states that the fact that one party paid the broker's fee is not determinative of whom the broker was representing.

126. **D** There is no required amount of license experience; any real estate licensee may be a dual agent. Fiduciaries are sometimes neutral (e.g., escrow agents), but a real estate agent is a fiduciary and is usually not neutral. Dual agencies are permitted provided the agent has the prior approval and knowledge of both parties and has given each party the required disclosed limited agency disclosure form.

127. **D** A dual agency must always be disclosed. Failure to do so violates the law of agency, and is also a violation of the Real Estate License Law. There is no distinction for different types of properties or transactions.

128. **C** When you buy property you have listed, you are already acting as the agent of the seller by virtue of the listing agreement, and you cannot deny that you are also representing your own interests. Therefore, an agent who buys his or her own listing is clearly at least a dual agent. A better practice would be to withdraw temporarily from the agency with the seller while negotiating on your own behalf as buyer.

129. **C** Most exchange agreements contain a provision that the agent is a dual agent of both or all parties to the exchange. It is also common, however, especially when there are two brokers involved, for each broker to have a listing on one of the properties, and perform as a single agent for one of the principals.

130. **C** Most exchange agreements contain a provision that the agent is a dual agent of both or all parties to the exchange. If there are two brokers involved, each can act as a single agent, but when both properties are listed by the same agent, there is no alternative than to be a dual agent. Dual agencies are permitted provided the broker has the prior knowledge and permission of both parties and gives the parties each the disclosed limited agency disclosure form required by the License Law and Administrative Rules.

131. **C** Compensation from both parties is never permitted without full disclosure to and consent from both parties. A listing agreement may or may not contain consent, but even if it does, it does not create full disclosure. The License Law states that accepting compensation from a party is not determinative of whom the broker represents.

132. **C** The agent owes a fiduciary duty to the principal, but also owes a duty to third parties of fair and honest dealings, competence and full disclosure of material latent defects. In this case, the agent owes the bank a duty of honesty and full disclosure which the agent has not honored. It is a material fact to the bank that the earnest money is a note and not collected funds.

133. **C** A broker can work alone or be the agent of the principal broker under whom the broker is licensed. The amount of compensation is set by agreement between the parties. Since the broker acts as an independent contractor, any attempt by the state or any other organization to regulate the amount of the compensation would likely be a violation of anti-trust laws. Note that the listing agreement does set the amount of compensation the seller agrees to pay the principal broker. But the broker's commission is set by agreement between the broker and his or her principal broker.

Forms

Forms required by ORS Chapter 696 (Real Estate License Act), ORS Chapter 105 (Seller Disclosure), Administrative Rules Chapter 863, Division 15, (Regarding Agency Relationships)

OREGON REAL ESTATE AGENCY DISCLOSURE PAMPHLET

(OAR 863-015-215(4))

This pamphlet describes agency relationships and the duties and responsibilities of real estate licensees in Oregon. This pamphlet is informational only and neither the pamphlet nor its delivery to you may be construed to be evidence of intent to create an agency relationship.

Real Estate Agency Relationships

An "agency" relationship is a voluntary legal relationship in which a real estate licensee (the "agent") agrees to act on behalf of a buyer or a seller (the "client") in a real estate transaction. Oregon law provides for three types of agency relationships between real estate agents and their clients:

Seller's Agent – Represents the seller only;

Buyer's Agent – Represents the buyer only;

Disclosed Limited Agent – Represents both the buyer and seller, or multiple buyers who want to purchase the same property. This can be done only with the written permission of both clients.

The actual agency relationships between the seller, buyer and their agents in a real estate transaction must be acknowledged at the time an offer to purchase is made. Please read this pamphlet carefully before entering into an agency relationship with a real estate agent.

Duties and Responsibilities of an Agent
Who Represents Only the Seller or Only the Buyer

Under a written listing agreement to sell property, an agent represents only the seller unless the seller agrees in writing to allow the agent to also represent the buyer. An agent who agrees to represent a buyer acts only as the buyer's agent unless the buyer agrees in writing to allow the agent to also represent the seller. An agent who represents only the seller or only the buyer owes the following affirmative duties to their client, other parties and their agents involved in a real estate transaction:

1. To exercise reasonable care and diligence;
2. To deal honestly and in good faith;
3. To present all written offers, notices and other communications in a timely manner whether or not the seller's property is subject to a contract for sale or the buyer is already a party to a contract to purchase;
4. To disclose material facts known by the agent and not apparent or readily ascertainable to a party;
5. To account in a timely manner for money and property received from or on behalf of the client;
6. To be loyal to their client by not taking action that is adverse or detrimental to the client's interest in a transaction;
7. To disclose in a timely manner to the client any conflict of interest, existing or contemplated;
8. To advise the client to seek expert advice on matters related to the transactions that are beyond the agent's expertise;
9. To maintain confidential information from or about the client except under subpoena or court order, even after termination of the agency relationship; and
10. When representing a seller, to make a continuous, good faith effort to find a buyer for the property, except that a seller's agent is not required to seek additional offers to purchase the property while the property is subject to a contract for sale. When representing a buyer, to make a continuous, good faith effort to find property for the buyer, except that a buyer's agent is not required to seek addition-

Agency disclosure pamphlet. Real estate agents are required to give a copy to each prospective buyer and seller at the time of first contact, unless the buyer or seller already has one.

al properties for the buyer while the buyer is subject to a contract for purchase or to show properties for which there is no written agreement to pay compensation to the buyer's agent. None of these affirmative duties of an agent may be waived, except #10, which can only be waived by written agreement between client and agent.

Under Oregon law, a seller's agent may show properties owned by another seller to a prospective buyer and may list competing properties for sale without breaching any affirmative duty to the seller. Similarly, a buyer's agent may show properties in which the buyer is interested to other prospective buyers without breaching any affirmative duty to the buyer.

Unless agreed to in writing, an agent has no duty to investigate matters that are outside the scope of the agent's expertise.

Duties and Responsibilities of an Agent
Who Represents More than One Client in a Transaction

One agent may represent both the seller and the buyer in the same transaction, or multiple buyers who want to purchase the same property only under a written "Disclosed Limited Agency" agreement, signed by the seller, buyer(s) and their agent. When different agents associated with the same real estate firm establish agency relationships with different parties to the same transaction, only the principal broker (the broker who supervises the other agents) will act as a Disclosed Limited Agent for both the buyer and seller. The other agents continue to represent only the party with whom the agent already has an established agency relationship unless all parties agree otherwise in writing. The supervising broker and the agents representing either the seller or the buyer have the following duties to their clients:

1. To disclose a conflict of interest in writing to all parties;
2. To take no action that is adverse or detrimental to either party's interest in the transaction; and
3. To obey the lawful instruction of both parties.

An agent acting under a Disclosed Limited Agency agreement has the same duties to the client as when representing only a seller or only a buyer, except that the agent may not, without written permission, disclose any of the following:

1. That the seller will accept a lower price or less favorable terms than the listing price or terms;
2. That the buyer will pay a greater price or more favorable terms than the offering price or terms; or
3. In transactions involving one-to-four residential units only, information regarding the real property transaction including, but not limited to, price, terms, financial qualifications or motivation to buy or sell.

No matter whom they represent, an agent *must* disclose information the agent knows or should know that failure to disclose would constitute fraudulent misrepresentation. Unless agreed to in writing, an agent acting under a Disclosed Limited Agency agreement has no duty to investigate matters that are outside the scope of the agent's expertise.

You are encouraged to discuss the above information with the agent delivering this pamphlet to you. If you intend for that agent, or any other Oregon real estate agent, to represent you as a Seller's Agent, Buyer's Agent, or Disclosed Limited Agent, you should have a specific discussion with him/her about the nature and scope of the agency relationship. Whether you are a buyer or seller, you cannot make a licensee your agent without their knowledge and consent, and an agent cannot make you their client without your knowledge and consent.

Property Address _____

Addendum to Listing Agreement Dated _____

Real Estate Firm _____

DISCLOSED LIMITED AGENCY AGREEMENT FOR SELLER

The Parties to this Disclosed Limited Agency Agreement are:

Listing Agent (print) _____

Listing Agent's Principal Broker (print) _____

Seller (print) _____

Seller (print) _____

The Parties to this Agreement understand that Oregon law allows a single real estate agent to act as a disclosed limited agent – to represent both the seller and the buyer in the same real estate transaction, or multiple buyers who want to purchase the same property. It is also understood that when different agents associated with the same principal broker (the broker who directly supervises the other agents) establish agency relationships with the buyer and seller in a real estate transaction, the agents' principal broker shall be the only broker acting as a disclosed limited agent representing both seller and buyer. The other agents shall continue to represent only the party with whom they have an established agency relationship, unless all parties agree otherwise in writing.

In consideration of the above understanding, and the mutual promises and benefits exchanged here and in the Listing Agreement, the Parties now agree as follows:

1. Seller acknowledge they have received the initial agency disclosure pamphlet required by ORS 696.820 and have read and discussed with the Listing Agent that part of the pamphlet entitled "Duties and Responsibilities of an Agent Who Represents More than One Party to a Transaction." The initial agency disclosure pamphlet is hereby incorporated into this Disclosed Limited Agency Agreement by reference.

2. Seller, having discussed with the Listing Agent the duties and responsibilities of an agent who represents more than one party to a transaction, consent and agree as follows:

   (A) The Listing Agent and the Listing Agent's Principal Broker, in addition to representing Seller, may represent one or more buyers in a transaction involving the listed property;

   (B) In a transaction involving the listed property where the buyer is represented by an agent who works in the same real estate business as the Listing Agent and who is supervised by the Listing Agent's Principal Broker, the Principal Broker may represent both Seller and Buyer. In such a situation, the Listing Agent will continue to represent only the Seller and the other agent will represent only the Buyer, consistent with the applicable duties and responsibilities as set out in the initial agency disclosure pamphlet; and

   (C) In all other cases, the Listing Agent and the Listing Agent's Principal Broker shall represent Seller exclusively.

Seller signature _____ Date _____

Seller signature _____ Date _____

Listing Agent signature _____ Date _____

(On their own and on behalf of Principal Broker)

Broker initial and review date _____

Disclosed Limited Agency Agreement for seller. When an agent wishes to represent both a buyer and a seller as a dual agent it is called a disclosed limited agency, and this is the form that must be given to the seller.

Property Address _____

Addendum to Buyer Service Agreement Dated _____

Real Estate Firm _____

DISCLOSED LIMITED AGENCY AGREEMENT FOR BUYER

The Parties to this Disclosed Limited Agency Agreement are:

Buyer's Agent (print) _____

Buyer's Agent's Principal Broker (print) _____

Buyer (print) _____

Buyer (print) _____

The Parties to this Agreement understand that Oregon law allows a single real estate agent to act as a disclosed limited agent – to represent both the seller and the buyer in the same real estate transaction, or multiple buyers who want to purchase the same property. It is also understood that when different agents associated with the same principal broker (the broker who directly supervises the other agents) establish agency relationships with the buyer and seller in a real estate transaction, the agents' principal broker shall be the only broker acting as a disclosed limited agent representing both seller and buyer. The other agents shall continue to represent only the party with whom they have an established agency relationship, unless all parties agree otherwise in writing.

In consideration of the above understanding, and the mutual promises and benefits exchanged here and, if applicable, in the Buyer Service Agreement, the Parties now agree as follows:

1. Buyer(s) acknowledge they have received the initial agency disclosure pamphlet required by ORS 696.820 and have read and discussed with the Buyers Agent that part of the pamphlet entitled "Duties and Responsibilities of an Agent Who Represents More than One Party to a Transaction." The initial agency disclosure pamphlet is hereby incorporated into this Disclosed Limited Agency Agreement by reference.

2. Buyer(s), having discussed with Buyers Agent the duties and responsibilities of an agent who represents more than one party to a transaction, consent and agree as follows:

   (A) Buyers Agent and the Buyers Agent's Principal Broker, in addition to representing Buyer, may represent the seller or another buyer in any transaction involving Buyer;

   (B) In a transaction where the seller is represented by an agent who works in the same real estate business as the Buyers Agent and who is supervised by the Buyers Agent's Principal Broker, the Principal Broker may represent both seller and Buyer. In such a situation, the Buyers Agent will continue to represent only the Buyer and the other agent will represent only the Seller, consistent with the applicable duties and responsibilities set out in the initial agency disclosure pamphlet;

   (C) In all other cases, the Buyers Agent and the Buyers Agent's Principal Broker shall represent Buyer exclusively.

Buyer signature _____ Date _____

Buyer signature _____ Date _____

Buyer's Agent signature _____ Date _____

(On their own and on behalf of Principal Broker)

Broker initial and review date _____

Disclosed Limited Agency Agreement for seller. When an agent wishes to represent both a buyer and a seller as a dual agent it is called a disclosed limited agency, and this is the form that must be given to the buyer.

FINAL AGENCY ACKNOWLEDGEMENT

Both Buyer and Seller acknowledge having received the Oregon Real Estate Agency Disclosure Pamphlet, hereby acknowledge and consent to the following agency relationships in this transaction:

(1)

_____ (Name of Selling Licensee) of

_____ (Name of Real Estate Firm) is the agent of

(check one)

❑ The Buyer exclusively.

❑ The Seller exclusively (Seller Agency").

❑ Both the Buyer and the Seller ("Disclosed Limited Agency").

(2)

_____ (Name of Listing Licensee) of

_____ (Name of Real Estate Firm) is the agent of

(check one)

❑ The Seller exclusively.

❑ Both the Buyer and the Seller ("Disclosed Limited Agency").

(3) If both parties are each represented by one or more licensees in the same real estate firm, and the licensees are supervised by the same principal broker in that real estate firm, Buyer and Seller acknowledge that said principal broker shall become the disclosed limited agent for both Buyer and Seller as more fully explained in the disclosed Limited Agency Agreements that have been reviewed and signed by Buyer, Seller and Licensee(s).

Buyer shall sign this acknowledgment at the time of signing this Agreement before submission to Seller. Seller shall sign this acknowledgment at the time this Agreement is first submitted to Seller, even if this Agreement will be rejected or a counter offer will be made. Sellers signature to this Final Agency Acknowledgment shall not constitute acceptance of the Agreement or any terms therein.

ACKNOWLEDGED

Buyer: _____

Print _____ Dated: _____

Buyer: _____

Print _____ Dated: _____

Seller: _____

Print _____ Dated: _____

Seller: _____

Print _____ Dated: _____

Agency acknowledgment language required for earnest money agreement or as addendum to earnest money agreement by amendment to Administrative Rule 863.200 adopted January 1, 2004. Most standard forms incorporate this language into the form. If the language is included in the earnest money agreement it must be at the top of the first page. If in a separate document it must also contain the property address and a reference to the earnest money agreement. In both cases it must be separately signed by the parties.

SELLER PROPERTY DISCLOSURE STATEMENT

Instructions to the Seller

Please complete the following form. Do not leave any spaces blank. Please refer to the line number(s) of the question(s) when you provide your explanation(s). If you are not claiming an exclusion or refusing to provide the form under ORS 105.475 (4), you should date and sign each page of this disclosure statement and each attachment.

Each seller of residential property described in ORS 105.465 must deliver this form to each buyer who makes a written offer to purchase. Under ORS 105.475 (4), refusal to provide this form gives the buyer the right to revoke their offer at any time prior to closing the transaction. Use only the section(s) of the form that apply to the transaction for which the form is used. If you are claiming an exclusion under ORS 105.470, fill out only Section 1.

An exclusion may be claimed only if the seller qualifies for the exclusion under the law. If not excluded, the seller must disclose the condition of the property or the buyer may revoke their offer to purchase anytime prior to closing the transaction. Questions regarding the legal consequences of the seller's choice should be directed to a qualified attorney.

(Do not fill out this section unless you are claiming an exclusion under ORS 105.470)

Section 1. Exclusion from ORS 105.465–105.490:
You may claim an exclusion under ORS 105.470 only if you qualify under the statute. If you are not claiming an exclusion, you must fill out Section 2 of this form completely.

Initial only the exclusion you wish to claim.

❑ This is the first sale of a dwelling never occupied. The dwelling is constructed or installed under building or installation permit(s) #_____ , issued by _____ .
❑ This sale is by a financial institution that acquired the property as custodian, agent or trustee, or by foreclosure or deed in lieu of foreclosure.
❑ The seller is a court appointed receiver, personal representative, trustee, conservator or guardian.
❑ This sale or transfer is by a governmental agency.

Signature(s) of Seller claiming exclusion _____

Date _____

Buyer(s) to acknowledge Seller's claim _____

Date _____

(IF YOU DID NOT CLAIM AN EXCLUSION IN SECTION 1, YOU MUST FILL OUT THIS SECTION.)

Section 2. Seller's property disclosure statement
(NOT A WARRANTY)
(ORS 105.465)

NOTICE TO THE BUYER: THE FOLLOWING REPRESENTATIONS ARE MADE BY THE SELLER(S) CONCERNING THE CONDITION OF THE PROPERTY LOCATED AT _____ ("THE PROPERTY").

DISCLOSURES CONTAINED IN THIS FORM ARE PROVIDED BY THE SELLER ON THE BASIS OF SELLER'S ACTUAL KNOWLEDGE OF THE PROPERTY AT THE TIME OF DISCLOSURE. BUYER HAS FIVE DAYS FROM THE SELLER'S DELIVERY OF THIS SELLER'S DISCLOSURE STATEMENT TO REVOKE BUYER'S OFFER BY DELIVERING BUYER'S SEPARATE SIGNED WRITTEN STATEMENT OF REVOCATION TO THE SELLER DISAPPROVING THE SELLER'S DISCLOSURE STATEMENT, UNLESS BUYER WAIVES THIS RIGHT AT OR PRIOR TO ENTERING INTO A SALE AGREEMENT.

FOR A MORE COMPREHENSIVE EXAMINATION OF THE SPECIFIC CONDITION OF THIS PROPERTY, BUYER IS ADVISED TO OBTAIN AND PAY FOR THE SERVICES OF A QUALIFIED SPECIALIST TO INSPECT THE PROPERTY ON BUYER'S BEHALF INCLUDING, FOR EXAMPLE, ONE OR MORE OF THE FOLLOWING: ARCHITECTS, ENGINEERS, PLUMBERS, ELECTRICIANS, ROOFERS, ENVIRONMENTAL INSPECTORS, BUILDING INSPECTORS, CERTIFIED HOME INSPECTORS, OR PEST AND DRY ROT INSPECTORS.

Seller ❑ is ❑ is not occupying the property.

I. SELLER'S REPRESENTATIONS:
The following are representations made by the seller and are not the representations of any financial institution that may have made or may make a loan pertaining to the property, or that may have or take a security interest in the property, or any real estate licensee engaged by the seller or the buyer.

*If you mark yes on items with *, attach a copy or explain on an attached sheet.

1. TITLE
A. Do you have legal authority to sell the property?　　　　　❑ Yes ❑ No ❑ Unknown
*B. Is title to the property subject to any of the following:　　❑ Yes ❑ No ❑ Unknown
　　(1) First right of refusal
　　(2) Option
　　(3) Lease or rental agreement
　　(4) Other listing
　　(5) Life estate?
*C. Are there any encroachments, boundary agreements, boundary
　　disputes or recent boundary changes?　　　　　　　　❑ Yes ❑ No ❑ Unknown
*D. Are there any rights of way, easements, licenses, access limitations
　　or claims that may affect your interest in the property?　❑ Yes ❑ No ❑ Unknown
*E. Are there any agreements for joint maintenance of an easement or
　　right of way?　　　　　　　　　　　　　　　　　　　❑ Yes ❑ No ❑ Unknown
*F. Are there any governmental studies, designations, zoning overlays,
　　surveys or notices that would affect the property?　　　❑ Yes ❑ No ❑ Unknown

*G. Are there any pending or existing governmental assessments
against the property? ❑ Yes ❑ No ❑ Unknown

*H. Are there any zoning violations or nonconforming uses? ❑ Yes ❑ No ❑ Unknown

*I. Is there a boundary survey for the property? ❑ Yes ❑ No ❑ Unknown

*J. Are there any covenants, conditions, restrictions or private
assessments that affect the property? ❑ Yes ❑ No ❑ Unknown

*K. Is the property subject to any special tax assessment or tax treatment
that may result in levy of additional taxes if the property is sold? ❑ Yes ❑ No ❑ Unknown

2. WATER

A. Household water

   (1) The source of the water is (check ALL that apply):
     ❑ Public ❑ Community ❑ Private ❑ Other _____

   (2) Water source information:

   *a. Does the water source require a water permit? ❑ Yes ❑ No ❑ Unknown

   If yes, do you have a permit? ❑ Yes ❑ No

   b. Is the water source located on the property? ❑ Yes ❑ No ❑ Unknown

   *If not, are there any written agreements for a shared water source? ❑ Yes ❑ No ❑ Unknown ❑ NA

   *c. Is there an easement (recorded or unrecorded) for your access to
     or maintenance of the water source? ❑ Yes ❑ No ❑ Unknown

   d. If the source of water is from a well or spring, have you had any of
     the following in the past 12 months?
     ❑ Flow test ❑ Bacteria test ❑ Chemical contents test ❑ Yes ❑ No ❑ Unknown ❑ NA

   *e. Are there any water source plumbing problems or needed repairs? ❑ Yes ❑ No ❑ Unknown

   (3) Are there any water treatment systems for the property? ❑ Yes ❑ No ❑ Unknown
     ❑ Leased ❑ Owned

B. Irrigation

   (1) Are there any ❑ water rights or ❑ other irrigation rights
     for the property? ❑ Yes ❑ No ❑ Unknown

   *(2) If any exist, has the irrigation water been used during the last
     five-year period? ❑ Yes ❑ No ❑ Unknown ❑ NA

   *(3) Is there a water rights certificate or other written evidence
     available? ❑ Yes ❑ No ❑ Unknown ❑ NA

C. Outdoor sprinkler system

   (1) Is there an outdoor sprinkler system for the property? ❑ Yes ❑ No ❑ Unknown

   (2) Has a back flow valve been installed? ❑ Yes ❑ No ❑ Unknown ❑ NA

   (3) Is the outdoor sprinkler system operable? ❑ Yes ❑ No ❑ Unknown ❑ NA

3. SEWAGE SYSTEM

A. Is the property connected to a public or community sewage system? ❑ Yes ❑ No ❑ Unknown

B. Are there any new public or community sewage systems proposed
for the property? ❑ Yes ❑ No ❑ Unknown

C. Is the property connected to an on-site septic system? ❑ Yes ❑ No ❑ Unknown

   If yes, was it installed by permit? ❑ Yes ❑ No ❑ Unknown ❑ NA

   *Has the system been repaired or altered? ❑ Yes ❑ No ❑ Unknown

   Has the condition of the system been evaluated and a report issued? ❑ Yes ❑ No ❑ Unknown

   Has it ever been pumped? ❑ Yes ❑ No ❑ Unknown ❑ NA

   If yes, when? _____

*D. Are there any sewage system problems or needed repairs? ❑ Yes ❑ No ❑ Unknown
E. Does your sewage system require on-site pumping to another level? ❑ Yes ❑ No ❑ Unknown

4. DWELLING INSULATION
A. Is there insulation in the:
    (1) Ceiling? ❑ Yes ❑ No ❑ Unknown
    (2) Exterior walls? ❑ Yes ❑ No ❑ Unknown
    (3) Floors? ❑ Yes ❑ No ❑ Unknown
B. Are there any defective insulated doors or windows? ❑ Yes ❑ No ❑ Unknown

5. DWELLING STRUCTURE
*A. Has the roof leaked? ❑ Yes ❑ No ❑ Unknown
    If yes, has it been repaired? ❑ Yes ❑ No ❑ Unknown ❑ NA
B. Are there any additions, conversions or remodeling? ❑ Yes ❑ No ❑ Unknown
    If yes, was a building permit required? ❑ Yes ❑ No ❑ Unknown ❑ NA
    If yes, was a building permit obtained? ❑ Yes ❑ No ❑ Unknown ❑ NA
    If yes, was final inspection obtained? ❑ Yes ❑ No ❑ Unknown ❑ NA
C. Are there smoke alarms or detectors? ❑ Yes ❑ No ❑ Unknown
D. Is there a woodstove included in the sale? ❑ Yes ❑ No ❑ Unknown
    Make _____
*E. Has pest and dry rot, structural or "whole house" inspection been
    done within the last three years? ❑ Yes ❑ No ❑ Unknown
*F. Are there any moisture problems, areas of water penetration, mildew
    odors or other moisture conditions (especially in the basement)? ❑ Yes ❑ No ❑ Unknown
    *If yes, explain on attached sheet the frequency and extent of prob-
    lem and any insurance claims, repairs or remediation done.
G. Is there a sump pump on the property? ❑ Yes ❑ No ❑ Unknown
H. Are there any materials used in the construction of the structure
    that are or have been the subject of a recall, class action suit,
    settlement or litigation? ❑ Yes ❑ No ❑ Unknown
    If yes, what are the materials? _____
    (1) Are there problems with the materials? ❑ Yes ❑ No ❑ Unknown ❑ NA
    (2) Are the materials covered by a warranty? ❑ Yes ❑ No ❑ Unknown ❑ NA
    (3) Have the materials been inspected? ❑ Yes ❑ No ❑ Unknown ❑ NA
    (4) Have there ever been claims filed for these materials by you or
        by previous owners? ❑ Yes ❑ No ❑ Unknown ❑ NA
    If yes, when? _____
    (5) Was money received? ❑ Yes ❑ No ❑ Unknown ❑ NA
    (6) Were any of the materials repaired or replaced? ❑ Yes ❑ No ❑ Unknown ❑ NA

6. DWELLING SYSTEMS AND FIXTURES
If the following systems or fixtures are included in the purchase price,
are they in good working order on the date this form is signed?
A. Electrical system, including wiring, switches, outlets and service ❑ Yes ❑ No ❑ Unknown
B. Plumbing system, including pipes, faucets, fixtures and toilets ❑ Yes ❑ No ❑ Unknown
C. Water heater tank ❑ Yes ❑ No ❑ Unknown
D. Garbage disposal ❑ Yes ❑ No ❑ Unknown ❑ NA
E. Built-in range and oven ❑ Yes ❑ No ❑ Unknown ❑ NA

F. Built-in dishwasher   ❑ Yes ❑ No ❑ Unknown ❑ NA
G. Sump pump   ❑ Yes ❑ No ❑ Unknown ❑ NA
H. Heating and cooling systems   ❑ Yes ❑ No ❑ Unknown ❑ NA
I. Security system: ❑ Owned ❑ Leased   ❑ Yes ❑ No ❑ Unknown ❑ NA
J. Are there any materials or products used in the systems and
    fixtures that are or have been the subject of a recall, class action
    settlement or other litigations?   ❑ Yes ❑ No ❑ Unknown
    If yes, what product? _____
    (1) Are there problems with the product?   ❑ Yes ❑ No ❑ Unknown
    (2) Is the product covered by a warranty?   ❑ Yes ❑ No ❑ Unknown
    (3) Has the product been inspected?   ❑ Yes ❑ No ❑ Unknown
    (4) Have claims been filed for this product by you or by previous
        owners?   ❑ Yes ❑ No ❑ Unknown
        If yes, when? _____
    (5) Was money received?   ❑ Yes ❑ No ❑ Unknown
    (6) Were any of the materials or products repaired or replaced? ❑ Yes ❑ No ❑ Unknown

7. COMMON INTEREST
A. Is there a Home Owner's Association or other governing entity? ❑ Yes ❑ No ❑ Unknown
    Name of Association or Other Governing Entity _____
    Contact Person _____
    Address _____ Phone Number _____
B. Regular periodic assessments: $ _____ per ❑ Month ❑ Year ❑ Other _____
*C. Are there any pending or proposed special assessments? ❑ Yes ❑ No ❑ Unknown
D. Are there shared "common areas" or joint maintenance agreements
    for facilities like walls, fences, pools, tennis courts, walkways or
    other areas co-owned in undivided interest with others? ❑ Yes ❑ No ❑ Unknown
E. Is the Home Owner's Association or other governing entity a party to
    pending litigation or subject to an unsatisfied judgment? ❑ Yes ❑ No ❑ Unknown ❑ NA
F. Is the property in violation of recorded covenants, conditions and
    restrictions or in violation of other bylaws or governing rules,
    whether recorded or not?   ❑ Yes ❑ No ❑ Unknown ❑ NA

8. GENERAL
A. Are there problems with settling, soil, standing water or drainage
    on the property or in the immediate area?   ❑ Yes ❑ No ❑ Unknown
B. Does the property contain fill?   ❑ Yes ❑ No ❑ Unknown
C. Is there any material damage to the property or any of the
    structure(s) from fire, wind, floods, beach movements, earthquake,
    expansive soils or landslides?   ❑ Yes ❑ No ❑ Unknown
D. Is the property in a designated floodplain?   ❑ Yes ❑ No ❑ Unknown
E. Is the property in a designated slide or other geologic hazard zone? ❑ Yes ❑ No ❑ Unknown
*F. Has any portion of the property been tested or treated for asbestos,
    formaldehyde, radon gas, lead-based paint, mold, fuel or chemical
    storage tanks or contaminated soil or water?   ❑ Yes ❑ No ❑ Unknown
G. Are there any tanks or underground storage tanks (e.g., septic,
    chemical, fuel, etc.) on the property?   ❑ Yes ❑ No ❑ Unknown
H. Has the property ever been used as an illegal drug manufacturing or
    distribution site?   ❑ Yes ❑ No ❑ Unknown
    *If yes, was a Certificate of Fitness issued?   ❑ Yes ❑ No ❑ Unknown

9. FULL DISCLOSURE BY SELLERS

*A. Are there any other material defects affecting this property or its
value that a prospective buyer should know about? ❏ Yes ❏ No
*If yes, describe the defect on attached sheet and explain the
frequency and extent of the problem and any insurance claims,
repairs or remediation.

B. Verification:

The foregoing answers and attached explanations (if any) are complete and correct to the best of my/our
knowledge and I/we have received a copy of this disclosure statement. I/we authorize my/our agents to deliver a copy of this disclosure statement to all prospective buyers of the property or their agents.

Seller(s) signature:

SELLER _____ DATE _____

SELLER _____ DATE _____

II. BUYER'S ACKNOWLEDGMENT

A. As buyer(s), I/we acknowledge the duty to pay diligent attention to any material defects that are known
to me/us or can be known by me/us by utilizing diligent attention and observation.

B. Each buyer acknowledges and understands that the disclosures set forth in this statement and in any
amendments to this statement are made only by the seller and are not the representations of any financial
institution that may have made or may make a loan pertaining to the property, or that may have or take a
security interest in the property, or of any real estate licensee engaged by the seller or buyer. A financial institution or real estate licensee is not bound by and has no liability with respect to any representation, misrepresentation, omission, error or inaccuracy contained in another party's disclosure statement required by
this section or any amendment to the disclosure statement.

C. Buyer (which term includes all persons signing the "buyer's acknowledgment" portion of this disclosure
statement below) hereby acknowledges receipt of a copy of this disclosure statement (including attachments, if any) bearing seller's signature(s).

DISCLOSURES, IF ANY, CONTAINED IN THIS FORM ARE PROVIDED BY THE SELLER ON THE BASIS OF SELLER'S
ACTUAL KNOWLEDGE OF THE PROPERTY AT THE TIME OF DISCLOSURE. IF THE SELLER HAS FILLED OUT
SECTION 2 OF THIS FORM, YOU, THE BUYER, HAVE FIVE DAYS FROM THE SELLER'S DELIVERY OF THIS DIS-
CLOSURE STATEMENT TO REVOKE YOUR OFFER BY DELIVERING YOUR SEPARATE SIGNED WRITTEN STATE-
MENT OF REVOCATION TO THE SELLER DISAPPROVING THE SELLER'S DISCLOSURE UNLESS YOU WAIVE THIS
RIGHT AT OR PRIOR TO ENTERING INTO A SALE AGREEMENT.

BUYER HEREBY ACKNOWLEDGES RECEIPT OF A COPY OF THIS SELLER'S PROPERTY DISCLOSURE STATEMENT.

BUYER _____ DATE _____

BUYER _____ DATE _____

Agent receiving disclosure statement on buyer's behalf to sign and date:

Real Estate Licensee _____

Real Estate Firm _____

Date received by agent _____

Agency Case Studies

The case studies on the following pages are designed to be discussed in a classroom setting. They are meant to provoke thought and even a bit of argument to clarify real-world agency issues. Most of the time there is a clear correct answer or outcome, but some cases are subject to interpretation of the exact events. Therefore, some students may come up with different answers that are correct based on what they assumed about the situation.

If you are studying this text on your own you will find a discussion of each case study following the case studies.

Agency Case Study 1

Broker Upton O'Goode took a listing on a residence. One of O'Goode's old college friends has asked to see the property. O'Goode made disclosure to the buyer that he is representing the seller and then showed the property to the buyer. After seeing the property the buyer decided to make an offer.

1. When O'Goode presents the offer to the seller, should he say anything about his friendship with the buyer? Why or why not? (Explain your reasoning.)

2. Suppose O'Goode and the buyer were close friends. Would O'Goode need to disclose the friendship to the seller when presenting the offer? Why or why not? (Explain your reasoning.)

3. Would O'Goode need to disclose to the seller if the buyer was related to him by blood or marriage instead? Why or why not? (Explain your reasoning.)

4. Suppose O'Goode was not the buyer's friend or related to the buyer, but has sold twelve houses to the buyer during the preceding year, although never as a buyer's agent. Would he have to disclose this to the seller when presenting the offer? Why or why not? (Explain your reasoning.)

Agency Case Study 2

Broker Sam Fastpen took a listing on a house which had an assumable loan. A buyer approached Sam and asked to see the property. Sam made disclosure to the buyer that he was representing the seller and not the buyer. During the showing the buyer asked questions about the neighborhood, the schools in the area, amount of the annual property taxes on the house and how much Sam thought it would cost for annual insurance premiums. Sam answered all these questions truthfully to the best of his ability. The buyer also asked if the loan was assumable and, if so, what the remaining balance and interest rate were. Sam disclosed this information to the buyer also. Finally, the buyer asked how low the seller would go. Sam replied that he didn't know but that he felt the seller was motivated to sell.

1. Has Sam Fastpen violated his obligations to the seller? To the buyer? Why or why not? (Explain your reasoning.)

2. If Sam was representing the buyer instead of the seller, would any of his actions have violated his obligations to the buyer? To the seller? Why or why not? (Explain your reasoning.)

Agency Case Study 3

Broker Betty Byzit approached a for sale by owner to ask for a listing. The sellers indicated a willingness to list the property, but wanted Betty to add the commission to the $285,000 price that the sellers had been asking. Prior to the listing appointment Betty had prepared a competitive market analysis for the property which indicated it should be listed at approximately $250,000. Without specifically showing the competitive market analysis data to the sellers, Betty indicated that she felt $285,000 plus the commission would be too high but that she and her company would try if the sellers would give her the listing. The sellers agreed and Betty listed the property for $305,000 for a one-year term. Betty then placed a for sale sign on the property and entered the listing in the multiple listing service. However, she did not advertise the property because she felt it was overpriced.

After three months with no offers the sellers notified Betty and her company that they were cancelling the listing. The company replied that if the sellers wished to cancel the listing they would have to pay the company's expenses incurred up to that time.

1. Can the sellers cancel the listing? If so, must they pay the company's expenses? Why or why not? (Explain your reasoning.)

2. Do Betty or her company have any liability to the sellers? Why or why not? (Explain your reasoning.)

Agency Case Study 4

Fred Leafticker is a sole proprietor broker located in Medford who specializes in apartment complexes. He took a six-month listing on a single-family residence in Portland. Because he does not have an office in Portland and knows little of the market for single-family residences, he contacted residential brokers in the Portland area and offered to co-broker the listing with them on terms typical for cooperative sales in Portland. Not being a member of the local multiple listing service he was unable to place it in the multiple, but he felt that his direct contact with local brokers was just as effective. He did not travel to Portland to view the property, nor did he have a for sale sign placed on it.

During the first month of the listing Fred did not advertise the property and it was not shown to any prospective buyers. The sellers then notified Fred that they were canceling the listing. Fred responded that if they canceled the listing they would have to pay him the full commission. The sellers replied that he would have to sue them for it and, if he did, they would countersue for damages caused by his failure to sell the property.

1. Can the sellers cancel the listing? If so, must they pay the commission? Why or why not? (Explain your reasoning.)

2. Do the sellers have cause of action against the broker for damages? What if his failure to find a buyer caused them to lose another house they were making an offer on and resulted in forfeiture of earnest money they put down on it? Why or why not? (Explain your reasoning.)

·

Agency Case Study 5

Frank Lee Dumm was a broker licensed under Barry Beanhead, the principal broker for Optimism Associates, Incorporated. Frank took a six-month listing on a rental property owned by the Great Bux Corporation. As soon as it was listed Frank turned the listing in to Barry Beanhead who, in turn, placed it in the local multiple listing service and ordered a for sale sign placed on the property. However, within a week of taking the listing, and without ever advertising the property for sale other than the for sale sign on the property, Frank transferred his license to another principal broker.

As soon as Frank transferred his license Barry Beanhead decided to work Frank's listing himself rather than assign it to another broker in the company. His employment agreement with Frank stated that if Frank left the company he would not be able to take his listings with him and would not be entitled to any portion of the commissions if they were sold. Thus Barry Beanhead would be entitled to keep the full commission.

For the next several weeks Barry Beanhead was busy running the company and did not pay attention to the listing. It was not advertised and not shown to any prospective buyers. At the end of the fifth week of the listing the seller instructed Barry Beanhead to discontinue working on selling the property as they were canceling the listing because Optimism Associates, Inc. was doing a poor job of selling it.

1. Has Frank Lee Dumm violated his fiduciary obligations to the Great Bux Corporation? Has Barry Beanhead? Why or why not? (Explain your reasoning.)

2. Can the Great Bux Corporation cancel the listing? If so, would they be liable for damages to Optimism Assocaites, Inc.? If so, how much would the damages likely be? Why or why not? (Explain your reasoning.)

Agency Case Study 6

Helen Weels is a real estate broker for Realty Marketers, Inc. She took a listing on a residence for $300,000, which was market value. At the time of taking the listing the seller explained that financial distress forced the sale so the seller would take much less if necessary as long as a sale could be finalized within two months.

Helen placed a for sale sign on the property and turned the listing in to the local multiple listing service. She also placed a classified ad to run in the real estate for sale section of the local paper for the following weekend. The headline on the ad said "Desperate Seller — Submit Offer."

The ad was successful in attracting buyers, one of whom made an offer of $225,000. Since this was the only offer, the seller accepted it. A few weeks later the transaction closed without any other offers being received.

After closing the seller demanded $75,000 in damages from Helen and Realty Marketers, Inc., plus refund of the commission.

1. Has Helen or Realty Marketers, Inc. violated the terms of their relationship with the sellers? Why or why not? (Explain your reasoning.)

2. Is the seller entitled to damages? If so, how much? Why or why not? (Explain your reasoning.)

Agency Case Study 7

Percy Thrumpmorton is a sole proprietor broker. Percy has a listing on a luxury home in a desirable area for $550,000. Percy has shown the house to numerous buyers but none has made an offer so far.

Suddenly, Angela Fishback, a broker with a large real estate company in town, calls with an offer on Percy's listing. Angela explains that she is working as a subagent and not as agent of the buyers. The sellers are at work, so Percy arranges an appointment to present the offer with Angela that evening.

In the meantime Percy calls all the buyers he showed the house to previously. Knowing that the property will soon be gone, one of the buyers decides to make an offer. Percy writes up the offer and then calls Angela to tell her that there is now another offer to present that evening. Angela asks how much the offer is for but Percy refuses to tell her.

Angela then calls her buyers and tells them that another offer has been received. Their original offer was for the listed price, but in order not to lose the property the buyers decide to increase their offer to $20,000 above the listed price.

When both offers are presented that evening Angela learns that the offer from Percy's buyers was for only $525,000. Since the offer from Angela's buyers is $45,000 more, the sellers accept it. Following the presentation Angela calls her buyers and explains that their offer has been accepted. She also tells them the amount of the other offer. The buyers are furious and try to back out of the transaction. However, under threat of a suit for specific performance from the sellers, the buyers go ahead and consummate the transaction.

1. Is it acceptable for Percy to refuse to tell Angela the amount of the offer from his buyers? Why or why not?

2. Is anyone liable to the buyers for damages? If so, who, and for how much? Why or why not? (Explain your reasoning.)

3. Would the answer be different if Angela had been working as a buyer's broker? Why or why not? (Explain your reasoning.)

Agency Case Study 8

Sandi Beach is a sole proprietor real estate broker as well as a real estate investor. She has taken a listing on a house which she feels would make a good rental investment for her. The listed price is $175,000 and the listing is for a term of three months.

When she took the listing Sandi placed a for sale sign on it and entered it into the multiple listing service. However, during the first month of the listing she did not advertise or show it. At the end of the first month she met with the seller and presented her offer to buy it for $150,000. On the offer she added the statement "buyer herein is a licensed real estate broker acting as principal and not as agent of seller." She proceeded to tell the seller that considering that no offers had been received so far she felt that her offer represented fair market value and that the original listed price was clearly too high. Based on this the seller accepted her offer and the transaction was subsequently closed.

1. Has Sandi violated any of the provisions of the Real Estate License Act or Administrative Rules? If so, in what way? If not, why not?

2. Has Sandi violated her fiduciary obligations to the seller? Why or why not? (Explain your reasoning.)

3. If the property had been listed by another real estate company, would this make a difference in your response to (2) above? If the property had been a for sale by owner, would this make a difference in your response to (2) above? Why or why not? (Explain your reasoning.)

Agency Case Study 9

Broker Ted DeBaer took a listing and sold it to a married couple. Ted did not represent the buyers and disclosed this fact to them at their first encounter. Nor were the buyers represented by any other agent. The seller knew the listed price was $30,000 above market, but the buyers did not know this and agreed to pay it. The delighted seller accepted the couple's offer and the transaction closed.

Six months later the buyers called Ted and indicated a need to sell the property. They asked him to list it for them.

    1. Can Ted take the listing? If so, how should he handle it? If not, why not? (Explain your reasoning.)

    2. Does Ted have an legal liability to the buyers? Why or why not? (Explain your reasoning.)

Agency Case Study 10

Sally Forth has a listing on a residence in which the seller has agreed to carry a land sales contract. The listed price is $250,000, which is market value. Sue Everyman is a broker from another real estate company representing a buyer. Sue has obtained a full-price offer in which the seller is to carry a contract with 20% down. Both brokers are present when this offer is presented to the seller. Sue presents the offer and discloses to the seller that she is representing the buyers exclusively. She does not present any information about the buyer's credit history.

Sally feels this is adequate down payment for security and says nothing to seller about the buyer's credit rating and does not suggest the seller obtain a credit report. If a credit report had been obtained it would have shown that the buyer was currently under foreclosure on another property.

The seller accepts the offer and the transaction closes on March 12 with the first payment on the contract due on May 1. The buyer does not make any of the payments and the seller is forced to foreclose. It takes the seller six months to complete the foreclosure and the seller incurs legal expenses of $2,500.

Following the foreclosure the seller relists the property with Sally at the same price. A few weeks later a full-price all-cash offer is obtained which the seller accepts. The transaction closes according to the agreement.

1. Is Sally liable to the seller for damages? If so, how much? If not, why not? (Explain your reasoning.)

2. Is Sue liable to the seller for damages? If so, how much? If not, why not? (Explain your reasoning.)

3. Suppose that market conditions change and the property goes down in value so the seller is able to resell the property for only $225,000. Would your response to (2) or (3) above be different? Why or why not? (Explain your reasoning.)

Agency Case Study 11

April Showers is a broker for Primary Realty. On May 15 April took an exclusive right to sell listing on a residence at $325,000 with a 6% commission rate. The sellers are very private people so they requested no sign on the property and that the listing not be placed in the multiple listing service.

May Flowers is a broker for Alternative Realty, a company that offers creative solutions to real estate problems. May likes to do cold-calling in her listing farm area. On May 16 she happens to call the sellers of April's listing. Using her standard sales line she states that she is calling up and down the street to locate properties for sale because the area is currently very desirable to buyers and there are few properties available.

The sellers respond that they are glad to hear that because they are interested in selling. Sensing the opportunity for a listing, May makes an appointment to go see the home. She does not ask if it is currently listed, nor do the sellers volunteer that information.

When May arrives for the appointment she quickly determines that the fair market value of the property is probably about $325,000. However, she knows that a small increase above that amount would probably not adversely affect the marketability, and sellers like to hear higher prices, so she decides to tell them she can list it for $340,000. When the sellers hear this they are excited and agree to list the property with her on an exclusive right to sell basis at a 7% commission rate.

May returns to her office and turns the listing in to her principal broker. Then she calls all the buyers she has been working with to tell them of the new listing. One couple seems very interested and she makes an appointment to show the property to them later that day.

When she shows the property to the buyers they are thrilled with it. They agree to offer the full listed price of $340,000 and May writes up the contract. She takes the buyers home and then returns to present the offer to the sellers. The sellers accept the offer immediately. May calls the buyers from the sellers' house and tells them that their offer has been accepted.

May returns to her office and turns in the completed sales contract to her principal broker. Financing and closing arrangements are made the next day and the transaction is ready to close two weeks later. On the day before the parties were scheduled to sign May's principal broker receives a call from the escrow advising them that they have received a notice of demand for a 6% commission from Primary Realty.

1. How much does the seller owe and to whom? Why or why not? (Explain your reasoning.)

2. Have either April or May violated any obligations to the sellers? To the buyers? Why or why not? (Explain your reasoning.)

3. Have either April or May violated any obligations to the buyers? To the buyers? Why or why not? (Explain your reasoning.)

4. Have either April or May violated any obligations under the Real Estate License Act or Administrative Rules? Why or why not? (Explain your reasoning.)

Agency Case Study 12

Max Flintheart is a sole proprietor broker operating alone as Flint Realty, an assumed business name. Max took a listing on a property at $300,000 and is holding an open house. A married couple come to the open house but it does not meet their needs.

Max tells them that he has many other properties listed himself and can find even more properties listed by other brokers through the multiple listing service. He gives them the pamphlet explaining agency relationships required by the Real Estate License Act and Administrative Rules of the Real Estate Agency. Max makes no other mention of agency.

The buyers tell Max what they are looking for and agree to let Max find some other properties to show them. They make an appointment to meet Max at his office later that afternoon. When they arrive at the appointment Max has already selected several properties and made arrangements to show them to the buyers.

One of the properties Max shows them turns out to be perfect and the buyers fall in love with it. It is listed for $350,000 by another real estate company. Max tells them he feels that is a fair price so they tell Max to go ahead and prepare an earnest money agreement (offer) for the full listed price. Max does so and then hands his pen to the buyers to sign it. The buyers look over the agreement and note the portion which contains the agency acknowledgment which they are to sign separately as an addendum to the offer. They note that Max has prepared it indicating that he is representing the sellers as agent of the listing company.

The buyers express surprise at this, informing Max that they were under the impression he was working for them. They become angry because they feel Max was less than forthright with them. As a result they sign the offer but refuse to sign the acknowledgment of agency addendum. They hand the signed offer to Max along with a check for the earnest money and leave.

1. What should Max do with the offer? (Explain your reasoning.)

2. If Max presents the offer to the sellers and they accept it, will he have any liability to the buyers? Why or why not? (Explain your reasoning.)

3. Has Max violated any part of the Real Estate License Act or the Administrative Rules of the Real Estate Agency? If so, why? (Explain your reasoning.)

Agency Case Study 13

Fritz Futzputtle is a sole proprietor broker who took a listing on a duplex at $325,000. He advertised the property in the local paper and this has resulted in an inquiry from a couple who are interested in living in one unit and renting the other unit out for investment income. Fritz makes an appointment with the buyers to show the property to them.

When he meets the buyers at the showing he hands them the agency pamphlet required by the Real Estate License Act and Administrative Rules, but says nothing further about whom he represents, other than the fact that he was the one who took the listing and the fact that he is a sole proprietor broker working indpendently.

The buyers like the property and instruct Fritz to prepare an offer for $300,000. Fritz does so and fills out the agency acknowledgment in the earnest money agreement indicating that Fritz is representing the sellers and not the buyers. The buyers sign the earnest money and the addendum. Then they inform Fritz that they will go as high as the full listed price, if necessary.

1. Does Fritz have any legal liability to the buyers? Why or why not? (Explain your reasoning.)

2. What should Fritz tell the sellers when he presents the offer, if anything? Why? (Explain your reasoning.)

.

Agency Case Study 1 — Discussion

Among other duties of an agent to the principal, an agent owes a duty of full disclosure. Full disclosure includes any fact pertinent to the agency, including presenting all offers, making a complete accounting of all funds and property coming into the agent's possession. In real estate an agent has an obligation to disclose the fair market value of the property, the financial condition of the buyer (if known) and the form in which earnest money was taken (if a seller's agent), that a fee will be paid to another agent (e.g., in a coop transaction), the legal provisions of an offer, and any relationship the agent has with the other party to the transaction.

In the case of the relationship with the other party it must be disclosed regardless of how slight it is. Ask yourself, if you were the seller and you discovered the relationship after the transaction closed, would you wonder if your agent's loyalty to you might have been compromised because of the agent's pre-existing relationship with the other party? In practically every case you would have to answer that it would make you question your agent's loyalty. Therefore the agent must disclose practically any relationship.

Agency Case Study 2 — Discussion

An agent owes duties of full disclosure to the principal and also to the third party, but the items which must be disclosed are different. To the seller a listing broker must disclose all written offers, notices and communications, all material facts known by the agent, a complete accounting, and any conflict of interest the agent may have. To the buyer a listing agent must disclose material latent defects in the property known to the agent, but other matters that would compromise a listing agent's loyalty to the seller must be kept confidential. However, matters that are public knowledge may be disclosed without affecting the agent's relationship with the seller.

If the agent represents the buyer, then these obligations are reversed. Therefore, if the agent knows how low the seller will go, the agent would have to disclose it to the buyer.

Agency Case Study 3 — Discussion

Normally in a contract either party has the option of either specific performance or damages as a remedy when the other party breaches the agreement. However, an agency contract cannot be enforced by specific performance; that is, either party may cancel it at any time. Therefore, the only possible remedy is damages.

If a seller cancels a listing agreement wrongfully the broker is ordinarily entitled to the full commission on the theory that the broker could have earned it if the seller had not withdrawn the authority. However, in Oregon the broker is entitled only to expenses the broker has incurred up to the point where the seller withdrew the listing.

On the other hand, if the seller withdraws the listing with just cause, then the seller is not liable for any damages at all. Any breach of the agent's duties to the seller would be just cause for such revocation of the listing. So the issue is whether Betty has breached her obligations to the sellers.

One issue that the sellers can argue is that Betty failed to tell them the fair market value of the property. Her counter-argument is that she did indicate that $305,000 was too high, plus the sellers had been asking the market value themselves previously as for sale by owner, so clearly they already knew the fair market value of the property. It is likely that Betty's counter-arguments would prevail in court.

The only other issue the sellers can raise is failure of due diligence. Betty owes them the duty "to make a continuous, good faith effort to find a buyer for the property" [ORS 696.805 (2)(j)]. The question is, does the listing broker fulfill this duty merely by placing a for sale sign on the property and placing the listing in the multiple listing service? Is there a duty to advertise the property or make other efforts to locate a buyer? The likelihood is that a court would find Betty's actions to be sufficient and she has not violated her duty of due diligence to the sellers. However, if the circumstances were otherwise a court might come to a different finding. For example, what if the sellers had indicated a need for a fast sale? Such a situation might be construed by a court as giving her a higher duty to perform.

If a court does determine that she has failed any of her obligations to the sellers, then she would be liable for any damages the sellers suffered as a result. For example, the sellers might have made an offer on another property and because this property hasn't sold they might forfeit an earnest money deposit on the new property. In addition, if the agent breaches any of the agent's obligations to the principal, then the agent loses the right to demand compensation, even if the agent successfully performs the task.

Agency Case Study 4 — Discussion

An agency contract cannot be enforced by specific performance; that is, either party may cancel it at any time. Therefore, the only possible remedy is damages. If a seller cancels a listing agreement wrongfully the broker is ordinarily entitled to the full commission on the theory that the broker could have earned it if the seller had not withdrawn the authority. However, in Oregon the broker is entitled only to expenses the broker has incurred up to the point where the seller withdrew the listing.

On the other hand, if the seller withdraws the listing with just cause, then the seller is not liable for any damages at all. Any breach of the agent's duties to the seller would be just cause for such revocation of the listing. So the issue is whether Fred has breached his obligations to the sellers.

The only issue the sellers can raise is failure of due diligence. At common law of agency due diligence means that the agent cannot accept a task that the agent cannot perform and, if the agent accepts a task, the agent must perform it in a legal manner acceptable to the principal as quickly as possible. In this case the sellers have a strong argument that the agent could not reasonably have expected to be able to perform the task. A court would probably agree that this gives them the right to withdraw the listing without being liable for damages.

As for the agent's duty to perform, ORS 696.805 (2)(j) says the listing agent has a duty "to make a continuous, good faith effort to find a buyer for the property." The question is, does the listing broker fulfill this duty merely by contacting other agents in the area and offering to co-broker the listing? Is there a duty to advertise the property, place a for sale sign on it, or make other efforts to locate a buyer? The likelihood is that a court would find Fred's actions to be insufficient and he has violated his duty of due diligence to the sellers.

If a court does determine that he has failed any of his obligations to the sellers, then he would be liable for any damages the sellers suffered as a result. In addition, if the agent breaches any of the agent's fiduciary to the principal, then the agent loses the right to demand compensation, even if the agent successfully performs the task.

Agency Case Study 5 — Discussion

A listing agreement is the personal property of the broker. If it is taken by a broker working under a principal broker, then the principal broker is the owner of the listing. It is not only legal, but normal practice for an employment agreement between a broker and a principal broker to provide that if the broker leaves the company the listings must remain. It is also the norm for the broker not to receive the listing commission even if the listing sells after the broker leaves.

The issue is whether the seller can cancel the listing without liability. Agency agreements cannot be enforced by specific performance, so either side can cancel it at any time. However, if a party cancels the agency contract without just cause there may be liability for damages to the other party. In the case of a seller who cancels a listing without legal cause the agent can claim damages to the extent of expenses incurred up to the point of cancelation.

The only just cause to cancel the listing would be if the agent violated the agent's obligations to the principal. In this case study the only possible violation is failure of due diligence – not working to obtain a buyer. The issue is whether placing a for sale sign on the property and entering it in the multiple listing service are adequate or if a court would feel that the agent had a duty to advertise it as well. According to case law it is unlikely that a court would find that the agent in this case has failed to perform to the extent that canceling the listing is justified. Part of the reason is that many brokers do not advertise properties for the first few weeks of a listing in the hope that it will sell without the expense of advertising. The scenario here is not unusual. Therefore it is likely that the seller would be liable to the agent for expenses incurred up to the point of cancelation.

Agency Case Study 6 — Discussion

If an agent violates any of the agent's duties to the principal the agent loses the right to collect the agreed upon compensation and is also liable to the principal for damages caused by the agent's breach of the obligation.

One of the obligations of an agent is confidentiality. Placing an ad in the paper stating that the seller is desperate clearly violates the duty of confidentiality. In this case it cost the seller potentially the difference between the listed price and the price the buyer offered. Therefore, the agent would probably be found liable for damages to that extent.

Note that the agency agreement can state anything the parties wish. If the listing had specifically authorized the agent to disclose to the buyer the seller's reason for selling, then the agent would not have violated the obligation of confidentiality. A simple thing the agent could have done would have been to furnish the seller with a copy of the ad to get the seller's approval before running it. Once the seller gives the approval it adds the specific ad to the agent's authority.

Agency Case Study 7 — Discussion

An agent owes duties of loyalty, full disclosure and confidentiality to the principal. To the third party the agent merely owes fair and honest dealing and full disclosure. In the case of full disclosure to the third party the agent must disclose anything pertinent to the agency as long as it doesn't violate the agent's duty of confidentiality to the principal. For example, a seller's agent must tell the buyer about material latent defects in the property but cannot disclose the seller's financial affairs or reasons for selling.

When there are two brokers from different companies and each is representing the seller, then the listing agent is the seller's agent and the selling agent is the agent of the listing agent. Thus, the selling agent's obligations in this case study are to the seller, not to the buyers.

Since the selling agent is the agent of the listing agent, the listing agent has no obligation to tell her the amount of another offer. Even if he had done so, so she could not have revealed it to the buyers. In multiple offer situations it is customary for each agent to keep the amount of their offer secret until the presentation. This works to the benefit of the seller because it heightens the buyers' uncertainty and makes them want to offer more out of fear of being outbid.

If the selling agent had been representing the buyers it probably wouldn't have made much difference on this issue. The listing agent still has no obligation to tell the selling agent the amount of the offer from his buyers. Therefore the selling agent's buyers still wouldn't have known how much it was. However, she might have given them counsel as to how much to offer.

Agency Case Study 8 — Discussion

The Real Estate License Act and Administrative Rules require that an agent give a potential client the required pamphlet about agency at the first contact. Presumably the agent in this case study did so when she took the listing. An agent is also required to disclose when buying or selling that the agent has a license. In this case she not only did so right on the earnest money form, but further clarified that she was not acting as the seller's agent for purposes of this transaction. Therefore, there is no violation of the License Act or Administrative Rules.

An agent owes the duty of loyalty to the principal. By taking a listing she became the seller's agent and therefore owed loyalty above all others to the seller, holding the seller's interests above even her own. When she made her offer she ceased to be the seller's agent, so she no longer owed the seller the duty of loyalty during the transaction.

However, she did owe the seller loyalty prior to making the offer. And there is evidence that she deliberately failed to market the listing in order to save it for herself and, possibly, to make the seller more anxious and more amenable to a low offer that she was planning on making all along. If a judge agrees with this then she owes damages to the seller.

If the seller had been represented by another real estate company then the possibility that she set the seller up for a low offer becomes much more remote. If the seller was a for sale by owner then she never had any duties to the seller.

Agency Case Study 9 — Discussion

One transaction affects the attitudes of a buyer or seller toward a licensee, but has no bearing on the relationship between the customer and the agent for future transactions. The agent can represent a customer in one transaction and represent the customer's adversary in the next. Therefore the fact that a broker did not represent the buyers when they bought the house does not mean the broker cannot go ahead and represent them by taking a listing if they later decide to sell the property.

As long as a broker selling a property to a buyer did not represent the buyer and disclosed that fact before entering into negotiations, the fact that the buyer paid too much for the property does not create liability for the broker.

When listing the property the broker must disclose what its market value is, as that is a duty that a listing agent has to the seller. Finding out that the broker induced them to pay too much for the property may cause the sellers to become angry and refuse to list with the broker, but the broker has no choice but to disclose the fair market value of the property.

Agency Case Study 10 — Discussion

A listing agent has a duty to disclose to the seller any material fact which the agent knows and to counsel the seller to seek the advice of others when such advise would be wise. This is required by the common law of agency and by the Real Estate License Act and Administrative Rules as well.

An agent is liable to the principal for any damages the principal suffers as a result of the agent's breach of any of the agent's duties. In addition, if the agent fails in any of the agent's duties the agent loses the right to collect the agreed upon compensation.

Damages, however, are awarded only if the damaged party can demonstrate the amount of the damages. In this case the seller was able to resell the property for the same price, so there was no loss of the sales price. However, the agent would likely be liable to the seller for the seller's expenses in foreclosing, and for return of the commission earned on the first sale. Of course, if market values decline and the seller has to resell the property at a lower price, then there is demonstrable damage to the seller which the agent would likely be held liable for.

A buyer's agent has no duty to disclose to the seller anything about the buyer other than to present the buyer's offer. Therefore the buyer's agent in this case study would incur no liability for damages.

Agency Case Study 11 — Discussion

The Real Estate License Act and Administrative Rules provide that brokers cannot subject an owner to payment of two commissions for one sale if the owner relists the property with a different broker after the termination of an original listing. But in this case study that is not what happened. Instead, the seller gave two exclusive right to sell listings to two different brokers. Under an exclusive right to sell listing each broker is entitled to the full commission regardless of who sells it. The seller is, therefore, liable for the full commission to both brokers.

However, the seller would owe the commission only to one broker if either broker learned of the other's listing before the sale took place. The second broker cannot take a listing knowing that it is already listed exclusively. In fact, if the second broker even had a hint that there might be an existing exclusive listing the second broker would have a duty to inquire.

But since there was no way for the second broker to know of the first listing, the sellers owe each the full commission. They may claim as an excuse that they did not know what they were doing, but ignorance of the law or of the language in a contract they signed will not excuse them.

In the real world this is extremely rare. The first broker would place a sign on the property and that would clearly indicate to the second broker that there might already be a listing. Also the listing is normally placed immediately in the multiple listing service, which makes other brokers aware of it. And finally, few sellers are so ignorant that they would list exclusively with two different brokers at the same time.

Agency Case Study 12 — Discussion

As long as the offer is signed by the buyers it is a valid offer and the agent must present it to the seller. And if the seller accepts it the agent must communicate the seller's acceptance back to the buyer to ensure that the contract is valid and enforceable.

The Real Estate License Act and Administrative Rules require the agent to give the pamphlet on agency, and he did so. It also requires the earnest money agreement to contain a ratification of the agency relationship, and the earnest money agreement the agent prepared in this case study does contain the ratification. There is no specific requirement to tell the parties that he is not representing them. Therefore, the agent has not violated the License Act or Administrative Rules.

However, ORS 696.845 provides "at the time of signing an offer to purchase, each buyer shall acknowledge the existing agency relationships, if any. At the time a seller accepts an offer to purchase, each seller shall acknowledge the existing agency relationships, if any. An agent to the real property transaction shall obtain the signatures of the buyers and the sellers to the acknowledgment, which shall be incorporated into or attached as an addendum to the offer to purchase or to the acceptance." Thus the agent would appear to be in violation of the License Act. However, as long as the agent exerted his or her best efforts to obtain the signatures it is doubtful that any disciplinary action could be taken against the agent.

While the License Act and Administrative Rules do not specifically require that the agent do any more than hand the parties the agency pamphlet, most agents give them a formal disclosure form of some sort as well. The main reason is to prevent exactly this kind of scenario.

But another reason is to avoid liability to the buyers. Without a disclosure form signed by the buyers they could easily argue that he had become their agent because of his actions. An agency relationship can be formed without even being in writing. And if a court agrees that he has become the buyers' agent, and he is alread the seller's agent by virtue of the listing agreement, then he is in an undisclosed dual agency. He could, therefore, be held liable for damages to the buyers.

Agency Case Study 13 — Discussion

The buyers clearly did not read the agency pamphlet or, if they did, they did not grasp that a listing agent is not on their side and must disclose to the sellers anything they say. They must feel the agent in this case study is either representing them or is in a dual agency relationship where he can maintain their confidence.

However, they signed the acknowledgment indicating that he is a single agent for the seller. Ignorance of the law or the terms of a written contract is no excuse. They have no claim against the agent for damages.

Since the agent is representing the seller he must tell the seller what the buyers told him. This will probably result in a counteroffer at the full listed price and terms. And when he goes back to the buyers with this counteroffer they may suspect he told the seller what they said. The sale cojuld easily blow up at this point. Nevertheless, the agent has no choice but to tell the seller what the buyers said.

In practice the agent would have been much better off to have gone beyond merely giving the buyers the agency pamphlet and disclosing his agency in the acknowledgment in the earnest money form. Clearly he would have been better off to have explained the pamphlet to them at the beginning to be sure they understood he would have to repeat anything they said to the seller.

Oregon Case Law

In the following section are landmark cases decided by the Oregon Supreme Court and the Oregon Court of Appeals relating to real estate brokers and the law of agency.

In reading this section it is important to understand the difference between statutes and court decisions. Statutes are passed by the Oregon Legislature and signed into law by the Governor. A statute, however, is subject to interpretation by the courts. The courts also have the authority to declare a statute unconstitutional.

When one party to a real estate transaction brings suit against the other the case is filed in a county court. The court hears all the arguments, testimony, and observes the evidence presented, then renders its decision. This decision establishes a precedent – that is, if a similar case is presented in the future, the court must render the same decision.

The losing party may appeal the decision of the county court to the Oregon Court of Appeals. It is important to note that the Court of Appeals does not generally retry the case. Its sole function is to decide if the trial court erred in interpreting the law. Thus, any evidence or testimony must be presented at the original trial.

The loser in the Court of Appeals may file a further appeal to the Oregon Supreme Court. In the majority of cases the Supreme Court will refuse to hear the cases, allowing the decision of the Court of Appeals to stand.

A decision rendered by a county court is binding only on that court. Thus we frequently find differences in the way agency laws are interpreted in each of Oregon's 36 counties. But once a decision is rendered in the Court of Appeals or the Supreme Court it establishes the precedent statewide and is binding on all county courts.

Court cases make dry reading material. To make it more interesting we have presented the case first, as though you were reading the pleadings of the parties in court. At the end you are given the opportunity to decide how the case should be decided, using your knowledge of the law of agency learned in previous sections. At the end of this section is a summary of what the Court of Appeals or the Supreme Court decided in each case. You can compare your decision to theirs to see if you agree.

Cases

1

A seller called a real estate office and told the agent who took the call that he needed to sell his property, which was a house on 12 acres of land. The seller told the agent that his reason for selling the property was that he was recently divorced, living with his small son, and that he had been unable to work because of illness.

The agent, an employee of the broker who owned the company, filled out the listing form as to the information about the property, but did not have the seller sign it. Later she acknowledged that she "figured we had a listing even though it was just information when it is not signed by the man who called up." Subsequently the firm advertised the property in the paper and showed it about three times.

After a short while the seller called the broker to express concern about the fact that the property was not selling. The employing broker went out to look at the property and asked the seller if he would reduce the price. The seller suggested a price about 15% lower, but the broker indicated that he had other nicer properties that were selling for even less. He suggested that a price about 50% of the original asking price "would move it faster."

A few weeks later the broker prepared and took to the seller an earnest money agreement filled out for a price a little over half the original asking price. The earnest money agreement was not signed by a buyer. It contained language granting the broker "10 days time to get buyer's acceptance." The seller signed this agreement on the line for the seller's signature. The earnest money agreement also called for a 6% commission.

Three days later the broker called the seller and said they thought they had a buyer. The seller went to the broker's office at which time the broker told the seller that the broker was the buyer. The broker told the seller that he was obligated to sell the property because he had signed the earnest money agreement. With the seller in the office, the broker then filled out a new earnest money agreement for the same amount as the earnest money agreement the seller had previously signed, less the commission. The seller signed this earnest money agreement.

After the sale was closed the broker spent a sum equal to about 15% of the purchase price in painting and fixing up the house. Then the broker advertised the property for sale as two separate parcels, one with the house and four acres, and the other as eight acres of bare land. The broker sold both properties for a combined price equal to one-third again the amount of the original asking price when the broker first started trying to sell the property for the seller.

When the seller found out about the sale he sued to recover the difference in what the property eventually sold for and what he received from the sale to the broker, plus punitive damages in an equal amount. The broker's defense was that the broker had no obligation to the seller because there was no listing agreement, hence the normal fiduciary duties do not exist. The broker pointed out that there could not be an agency relationship because the Statute of Frauds requires an agency agreement to be in writing and signed by the party to be charged in order to be enforceable.

If you were the judge, how would you decide this case?

2

A seller owned a ranch in eastern Oregon which was heavily mortgaged. He decided to sell a portion and listed it with a real estate broker. The broker secured various offers, but for various reasons none of them were consummated.

The seller did accept the first of these offers, although it failed because the mortgagee refused to agree to its terms. Three months after the offer was made and failed the buyer made a loan to the seller which was to be repaid over four years, secured by a second mortgage on the ranch. At the time of this loan the seller gave the buyer an option to buy the property for approximately the same price as the buyer's offer had been, of which the down payment was to be a little under 20% and the balance was to be paid in annual installments, with additional language stating "full balance including interest to be cashed out within ten years from date of first payment." The amount of the installments called for in the option would normally have required 40 years to pay off the balance of the purchase price, and the seller was elderly.

Approximately one year after the loan from the buyer to the seller and the option, the buyer obtained an Oregon real estate license.

Two years after the loan from the buyer was made, at which point the seller had paid off half of it, the seller refinanced the ranch with a different lender on a new first mortgage loan. The amount of the refinance was sufficient to pay off the original first mortgage and also the second mortgage loan made by the buyer. The seller's attorney prepared a satisfaction of mortgage and a quitclaim deed for the buyer to sign in order to give the seller clear title and a first mortgage to the new lender. These documents were accompanied by a new option to buy with the same terms as the first option. This option was to be recorded after the new first mortgage. The buyer was to return the signed documents and the option to the title insurance company where the new loan was being closed.

About a week later the buyer delivered the signed satisfaction and quitclaim deed to the escrow along with the option for the seller's signature. However, the buyer had altered the option and left out the clause requiring payment in full within ten years. Subsequently, the seller went to the escrow and signed all the papers necessary to complete the transaction, including the option. The seller did not read the option.

Later the buyer went to exercise the option, whereupon the seller discovered the changed terms. The seller refused to consummate the sale and the buyer sued for specific performance of the option. [Note: Specific performance is a remedy in contract law where a party to the contract asks the court to order the other party to perform the contract as agreed.]

If you were the judge, how would you decide this case?

3

A seller signed a listing agreement with a real estate broker to sell her property. The broker told her that the fair market value of the property was $164,325. Relying on that advice she accepted an earnest money agreement brought to her by the broker for that amount. Prior to closing she discovered that the market value of the property was really $400,000, and therefore she refused to close the transaction.

When she refused to close the buyer sued for specific performance of the earnest money agree-

ment. The case was appealed all the way to the Oregon Supreme Court, which took over two years from the signing of the earnest money agreement before their decision was rendered. The Supreme Court ruled in favor of the buyer and she was forced to consummate the transaction with the buyer for the $164,325 price.

Subsequently she filed suit against the broker for negligence, fraud, breach of contract and unlawful trade practices. At trial the broker raised the defense that the statute of limitations for the relevant complaints is two years in Oregon, and the seller had failed to bring the action within the time limit.

If you were the judge, how would you decide this case?

4

A couple wished to purchase land with an ocean view on which to build their retirement home. The ocean view was of great importance in their selection. A real estate agent showed them a lot on a bluff overlooking the ocean. The buyers were provided with a map showing the subdivision which the lot was part of. The map showed an adjacent area below the bluff which was indicated as a future condominium development.

The agent had no knowledge of the condominium developer's plans, so she asked the owners of the condominium land and the future developers of it to come to her office to discuss their plans with her buyers. The developers were also the owners of the lot the buyers were interested in buying. The buyers asked them about what effect their planned condominiums would have on the view from the lot they were interested in. The developers told them "you don't have to worry about the condominiums ... they're not going to hurt your view" and "the only way you're going to see these is if you walk right up to the edge of that bluff there ... then when you look down ... you'll see a roof line or a roof outline and that's all you're going to see." At the time the developers said this they had already filed the architectural plans for the subdivision with the city. However, they did not show the plans to the buyers or tell them that they had already been created and filed. The buyers and the developers then signed an earnest money agreement for the subdivision lot which was subsequently consummated.

About a year later, after the buyers had begun construction on their home, they observed that the sellers had begun construction of the condominiums below their lot. The buyers were concerned so they went to the city and looked at the plans. The plans showed that the condominiums would be built to the edge of the beach on concrete piers and would extend 67 feet above the beach. At that point the buyers realized that the condominiums would impair their view of the ocean.

The buyers then filed suit for fraud and violation of the Unlawful Trade Practices Act. The sellers responded with the defense that the statements made by the sellers was an opinion, not a statement of fact, and therefore did not constitute fraud.

If you were the judge, how would you decide this case?

5

A broker took a one-year listing on a restaurant. The listing stated that the seller would pay the broker a commission if the broker was successful in bringing about a sale of the property at the listed price and terms or any other terms that the seller accepted. It also provided that the seller would be obligated to the broker for the full commission at the listed price in the event the seller withdrew the listing prior to its expiration date.

After 27 weeks the broker found a buyer who made an offer, but the offer was not at the listed price and terms. Upon presenting the offer the seller rejected it and withdrew the listing. In reliance on the language of the listing agreement the broker demanded the full commission. The seller refused to pay and the broker brought suit.

If you were the judge, how would you decide this case?

6

A real estate broker took a listing on a residential property. Subsequently, the broker procured an offer which the seller accepted. While showing the property the buyers asked where the lot lines were. The agent showed the buyers what she thought were the lot lines. After closing it was discovered that 30 feet of the front of the lot as shown by the broker actually lay within the street right of way; that the garage was within a 20-foot setback, making it in violation of local zoning; that the property was narrower than what the broker showed the buyers; and that part of the carport and a brick wall encroached on neighboring property.

The buyers sued the seller and the real estate broker for misrepresentation and violation of the Unfair Trade Practices Act (ORS Chapter 646). The seller denied the claims pointing out that the legal description of the property in the listing and other documents was accurate and the buyers therefore had notice of the dimensions. The seller also cross-claimed against the broker for indemnification in the event he was required to pay damages to the buyers. The broker raised the same defense as the seller, that is, that the legal description is what the buyers bought, therefore they had no right to rely on representations of the broker, who was not a surveyor and not an expert.

If you were the judge, how would you decide this case?

7

A broker took a listing from a married couple on the N½ of the S½ of a quarter section (40 acres). The sellers lived in Indiana, but the father of the husband lived on adjacent land and managed the undeveloped property for the sellers. The sellers implicitly authorized the father of the husband to assist the broker in determining the boundaries of the listed property. The father told the broker that the southern boundary of the parcel was approximately ten feet north of an old fence. In fact, the southern boundary was approximately 53 feet north of the fence.

The broker procured an offer from a buyer in which the sellers were to carry a land sales contract. The sellers accepted the offer and the transaction closed. Two and a half years after closing the buyers discovered the error in the property boundary and sued to rescind the contract on the grounds of misrepresentation as to the correct boundaries of the property. The sellers filed a cross-claim against the broker for return of the commission in the event the court should allow the buyer to rescind the contract and the broker cross-complained for attorney's fees under the terms of the listing agreement.

[Note regarding contract law: A *rescission* of a contract is a remedy where everyone gives everything back and the parties are returned to the position they were in before they entered into the contract, as though it never existed, as far as is practical to do so.]

If you were the judge, how would you decide this case?

Final decisions

1

The trial was held before a jury, which ruled in favor of the seller on both the claim for loss of the sales price and the claim for punitive damages. The broker appealed, claiming that the trial court should have dismissed the case because the Statute of Frauds clearly states that the agency agreement must be in writing.

The Oregon Court of Appeals agreed that a broker "stands in a fiduciary relationship with his client" and that the broker "must make a full and understandable explanation to the client before having him sign any contracts, particularly when the contracts are with the broker himself." The Court added that "the relationship casts upon the broker the burden of showing that there was a full and complete disclosure and that the broker did not reap a secret profit."

As to the broker's defense that no broker-client relationship existed because of the Statute of Frauds, the Court stated "a fiduciary relationship exists in all cases where there has been a special confidence reposed in one who in equity and good conscience is bound to act in good faith and with due regard to the interests of the one reposing the confidence." Noting that the Statute of Frauds requires the agency agreement to be in writing, the Court nevertheless quoted a 1932 case involving the Wisconsin Statute of Frauds where the court ruled "the purpose of the statute was not to relieve real estate agents from their obligations as agents, but to protect the public against frauds perpetrated by dishonest agents through falsely claiming oral contracts of agency when another agent effect a sale by which the landowner was subjected to claims for commission by two or more agents, and by falsely claiming agency and claiming a commission for procuring a purchaser when no bona fide purchase was in fact procured" (*Krzysko v. Gaudynski*).

The Court pointed out that if the broker is allowed to claim that no agency agreement existed the broker could make whatever misrepresentations he desired, withhold any information he had a duty to disclose, and fail to disclose that he was planning on buying the property. Thus the broker would be able to use the Statute of Frauds to perpetrate a fraud. The Court affirmed the trial court's award of judgment against the broker on both counts.

Starkweather v. Schaffer, 262 Or 198 (1972)

2

The trial court found in favor of the seller and denied the buyer's suit for specific performance. The buyer appealed.

The Court of Appeals noted that the buyer had obtained a real estate license approximately one year before the option which was the subject of the suit was executed by the seller. However, the Court also noted that there did not exist a broker-client relationship between the buyer and the seller.

Normally this would mean that the buyer owed no fiduciary obligations to the seller. However, the Court further noted that the Real Estate License Act subjects a licensee to disciplinary action who "committed any act or conduct, whether of the same or of a different character, specified in this section which constitutes or demonstrates bad faith or dishonest or fraudulent dealings" [ORS 696.301 (31)]. The Court also noted ORS 696.020 (2) which states "a real estate licensee shall be bound by and subject to the requirements of ORS 696.010 to 696.495, 696.600 to 696.785, 696.800 to 696.855, 696.990 and 696.995 in engaging in any professional real estate activity or while acting in the licensee's own behalf in the offer to, negotiations for, or sale, exchange, lease option or purchase of real estate." In other words, the Court felt that the Legislature had extended the duty of fair dealing even to those transactions in which the licensee is one of the principals. Therefore, the Court ruled that the buyer was obligated to advise the seller that he had altered the terms of the option by deleting the 10-year payoff clause. While the Court noted that it is true that the seller should have read the documents, but the buyer's duty to disclose was foremost and, because he did not do so, he is not entitled to specific performance of the option.

Macdonald v. Dormaier, 272 Or 122 (1975)

3

The trial court found in favor of the broker on the grounds that the statute of limitations explicitly required that the seller file the suit within the two years and she failed to do so. The seller then appealed.

The Court of Appeals reviewed the case and considered the issue of exactly when the seller's claim against the broker began. If her complaint began at the time when she discovered that the market value of the property was $400,000, then she failed to file within the time prescribed by the statute of limitations. The Court noted her argument that she had no way to know if she was really damaged until the Supreme Court ruled against her and forced her to consummate the sale to the buyer. However, the Court disagreed with this position and affirmed the trial court's judgment in favor of the broker.

However one justice dissented and was joined in the dissent by three other justices. After all, had she been allowed to avoid performance of the earnest money agreement she would not have been seriously harmed by the broker's actions. The dissenting judges argued that her cause of action was provisional until the Supreme Court forced her to consummate the transaction, and therefore the statute should run from the decision of the Supreme Court, not from when she discovered the market value of the property. The dissenting opinion noted that court cases take some time to conclude and, if parties are forced to file claims for damages before the issue they are claiming under is finally determined, they create cross-conflicting cases where the parties have to defend themselves in one case and prosecute their position in the other, thus impeaching themselves. While this opinion was overruled, it is interesting to note that the broker escaped liability by a thread.

Jaquith v. Ferris, 64 Or App 508 (1983)

4

The trial was before a jury, which found in favor of the buyers. The sellers appealed, arguing that the judge should have ordered a directed verdict rather than let the jury decide, because the statements made by the sellers were clearly opinion which, as a matter of law, are not actionable. They also argued that the buyers had constructive notice of the plans because the real estate agents had complete plans and were the buyers' agents. Furthermore, they argued, the plans had already been filed and the buyers could have gone to the city to view them. Therefore, the sellers position was that the buyers had a duty to do so and, not having done so, cannot rely on the sellers' statements. If a buyer does not have a right to rely on a statement, then it cannot be construed as fraud.

The Court of Appeals agreed with the sellers that statements of opinion are not actionable as fraud, even though false. However, the Court quoted an earlier Oregon case which said "statements of

opinion regarding quality, value, or the like, may be considered as misrepresentations of fact, that is, of the speaker's state of mind, if a fiduciary relation exists between the parties ... or where the parties are not on an equal footing and do not have equal knowledge or means of knowledge" (*Jeska v. Mulhall*).

The Court noted that the parties were not on equal footing. The sellers certainly were familiar with the nature of the architectural plans, but the buyers did not even know the plans existed. Therefore, the Court concluded that it was proper for the trial court to allow the jury to decide whether the statements constituted fraud or not. As for whether the real estate agents were agents of the buyers or not, the Court noted that this was also a question of fact for the jury to determine.

As for whether the buyers had a duty to go to the city to view the plans, the Court noted that the buyers were not even told that the plans existed. Furthermore, they did inquire of the only source of information about the condominiums that they knew of, that is, the sellers, who knew that the plans existed and had been filed and failed to tell the buyers of these facts. The Court further noted that the buyers viewed the site and it appeared to them that it would be possible to build the condominiums without impairing their view. Thus, the buyers were given no reason to question the statements of the sellers and no reason to inquire further.

In short, the Court of Appeals affirmed the jury's decision in favor of the buyers and allowed their judgment to stand.

Haag v. Cembellin, 89 Or App 75 (1987)

5

The trial court found that the broker had not been damaged by the seller's withdrawal of the listing because the broker had failed to provide any evidence of damages. As for the contractual language requiring the seller to pay the full commission, the court felt that this was a penalty. Penalties in contracts are generally not enforceable. To be enforceable the court felt that the broker would have to present evidence that there was a likelihood that the property would have sold for the listed price and terms within the listing period. In other words, the broker should have provided evidence that the penalty clause was a reasonable attempt to forecast the harm the broker would suffer by the seller's breach in withdrawing the listing. Since there had been only one offer after 27 weeks, and that offer was not at the listed price and terms, it seemed unlikely that the broker would have been able to sell the property at all; thus the broker suffered no damages.

The broker appealed and the Oregon Court of Appeals affirmed the trial court's decision.

Dean Vincent, Inc. v. Krimm, 285 Or App 439 (1979)

6

The case was heard before a jury, which found in favor of the buyers for damages against the broker in the amount of $50,000 as general damages and $10,000 as punitive damages for violation of the Unfair Trade Practices Act, but denied the claim for misrepresentation. The court found the seller not liable on any of the buyers' claims. However, since the seller incurred legal expenses in defending herself, the court awarded the seller her costs as a judgment against the broker. The broker appealed, claiming that the amount of the damages should have been decided by the judge, not the jury, because the buyers presented no evidence as to the actual damages they suffered;, i.e., they did not present an appraisal indicating that the property was worth less than what they paid. The broker further claimed that the judgment in favor of the seller for her costs was improper because the seller had won against the claims of the buyers.

In reviewing the case the Court of Appeals ruled that the listing agreement provided for attorney's fees and costs to the prevailing party in the event of a suit. Although the seller successfully defended herself against the buyers, there was no language excluding an award of attorney's fees and costs in this situation, therefore the judgment against the broker for the seller's costs was proper.

As for the broker's argument that submitting the question of the amount of the damages to the jury was improper, the Court ruled that the question of whether the broker had violated the Unfair Trade Practices Act was a proper question for the jury to consider, therefore the Court declined to change their decision. However, the Court noted that the Unfair Trade Practices Act provides for actual damages or, if actual damages are not proved, a statutory amount of $200. Since the buyers did not present evidence of the amount of their actual damages, the Court ordered the award of $50,000 in general damages reduced to $200, but let stand the award of

$10,000 in punitive damages and the award of costs to both the seller and the buyers.

Martin v. Cahill, 90 Or App 332 (1988)

7

Citing earlier cases, the trial court ruled that any misrepresentation of the property boundary was grounds for rescission of the contract. The fact that the error was not discovered for two and a half years was irrelevant, since the statute of limitations on misrepresentation is two years from discovery, not two years from the beginning of the sale. The court ordered a rescission and also ordered the broker to return the commission to the sellers. All parties appealed the part of the trial court's decision which they lost.

The Court of Appeals agreed with the trial court that the rescission of the land sales contract was proper.

As to the broker's commission, the Court pointed out that the broker's misrepresentation to the buyers was innocent. The broker was relying on information from the father of one of the sellers, who had owned adjacent land for a long time. The father was evidently authorized to tell the broker where the boundaries lay and the broker was entitled to rely on the father's representations. Therefore, the Court reversed the trial court's order that the broker return the commission to the sellers. The Court further noted that the listing agreement contained language in which the seller's agreed to pay the broker's attorney's fees "in case of suit or action on this contract ... and appeal thereof." Since the broker had been involved in litigation as a result of the seller's failure to disclose the correct boundaries, it was proper for the broker to recover attorney's fees from the sellers.

West v. Georgi, 91 Or App 566 (1988)

Note the difference between *West v Georgi* above and *Martin v. Cahill* previously. In the former case the Court did not allow the broker the commission because the misrepresentation was the fault of the broker, not the seller. In *West v. Georgi* the source of the misinformation was the sellers and the broker merely innocently passed along the incorrect information.

Appendix

On the following pages you will find selections from the Oregon Real Estate License Act (ORS Chapter 696) and seller disclosure provisions of ORS Chapter 105. We have also included those Administrative Rules of the Oregon Real Estate Agency which relate to agency issues, and selected portions of the Oregon Unfair Trade Practices Act (ORS Chapter 646).

Note: The following excerpts from Oregon Revised Statutes Chapter 696 (the Real Estate License Act) have been edited from the version published by the Oregon Legislative Counsel. Changes were made to both chapters by the 2001 Legislative Session, but many of those changes have an effective date of July 1, 2002. Normally, changes to statutes become law 90 days after adjournment of the Legislature, which usually means they are effective sometime in the first half of October. Due to the unusual effective date of the changes the Legislative Counsel published the new statute, followed immediately by the old version of the same statute number. Since everyone reading this textbook will be doing so after July 1, 2002, we have deleted the old versions of the statutes and included only the new. All examination questions you may encounter will be based on the new statutes.

In addition, we have made changes mandated by Senate Bill 206 from the 2003 Legislative Session.

AGENTS' OBLIGATIONS

696.800 Definitions. As used in ORS 696.392, 696.600 to 696.785, 696.800 to 696.855 and 696.995, unless the context requires otherwise:

(1) "Agent" means:

(a) A real estate broker or principal real estate broker who has entered into:

(A) A listing agreement with a seller;

(B) A service contract with a buyer to represent the buyer; or

(C) A disclosed limited agency agreement; or

(b) A person licensed under ORS 696.022 who has entered into a written contract with a real estate broker or principal real estate broker to act as the broker's agent in connection with acts requiring a real estate license and to function under the broker's supervision.

(2) "Buyer" means a potential transferee in a real property transaction, and includes a person who:

(a) Executes an offer to purchase real property from a seller through an agent; or

(b) Enters into an exclusive representation contract or buyer's service agreement with a real estate broker or principal real estate broker, whether or not a sale or transfer of property results.

(3) "Confidential information" means information communicated to a real estate licensee or the licensee's agent by the buyer or seller of one to four residential units regarding the real property transaction, including but not limited to price, terms, financial qualifications or motivation to buy or sell. "Confidential information" does not mean information that:

(a) The buyer instructs the licensee or the licensee's agent to disclose about the buyer to the seller or the seller instructs the licensee or the licensee' agent to disclose about the seller to the buyer; and

(b) The licensee or the licensee's agent knows or should know failure to disclose would constitute fraudulent representation.

(4) "Disclosed limited agency" means a real property transaction in which the representation of a buyer and seller or the representation of two buyers occurs within the same real estate business.

(5) "Listing agreement" means a contract between a seller of real property and a real estate broker or principal real estate broker by which the broker has been authorized to act as an agent of the seller for compensation to offer the real property for sale or to find and obtain a buyer.

(6) "Listing price" means the amount expressed in dollars, specified in the listing agreement, for which the seller is willing to sell the real property through the listing agent.

(7) "Offer" means a written proposal executed by a buyer for the sale or lease of real property.

(8) "Offering price" is the amount expressed in dollars specified in an offer to purchase for which the buyer is willing to buy the real property.

(9) "Principal" means the person who has permitted or directed an agent to act on the principal's behalf. In a real property transaction, this generally means the buyer or the seller.

(10) "Real property" means any estate in real property, including a condominium as defined in ORS 100.005, a timeshare property as defined in ORS 94.803 and the granting of an option or right of first refusal. "Real property" also includes a mobile home or manufactured dwelling owned by the same person who owns the land upon which the mobile or manufactured home is situated. "Real property" does not include a leasehold in real property.

(11) "Real property transaction" means a transaction regarding real property in which an agent is employed by one or more of the principals to act in that transaction and includes but is not limited to listing agreements, buyer's service agreements, exclusive representation contracts and offers to purchase.

(12) "Sale" or "sold" refers to a transaction for the transfer of real property from the seller to the buyer and includes:

(a) Exchanges of real property between the seller and the buyer and third parties; and

(b) Land sales contracts.

(13) "Seller" means a potential transferor in a real property transaction and includes an owner:

(a) Who enters into a listing agreement with a real estate broker or principal real estate broker, whether or not a transfer results; or

(b) Who receives an offer to purchase real property, of which the seller is the owner, from an agent acting on behalf of a buyer.

696.805 Real estate licensee as seller's agent; obligations. (1) A real estate licensee who acts under a listing agreement with the seller acts as the seller's agent only.

(2) A seller's agent owes the seller, other principals and the principals' agents involved in a real estate transaction the following affirmative duties:

(a) To deal honestly and in good faith;

(b) To present all written offers, written notices and other written communications to and from the parties in a timely manner without regard to whether the property is subject to a contract for sale or the buyer is already a party to a contract to purchase; and

(c) To disclose material facts known by the seller's agent and not apparent or readily ascertainable to a party;

(3) A seller's agent owes the seller involved in a real estate transaction the following affirmative duties:

(a) To exercise reasonable care and diligence;

(b) To account in a timely manner for money and property received from or on behalf of the seller.

(c) To be loyal to the seller by not taking action that is adverse or detrimental to the seller's interest in a transaction;

(d) To disclose in a timely manner to the seller any conflict of interest, existing or contemplated;

(e) To advise the seller to seek expert advice on matters related to the transaction that are beyond the agent's expertise;

(f) To maintain confidential information from or about the seller except under subpoena or court order, even after termination of the agency relationship; and

(g) Unless agreed otherwise in writing, to make a continuous, good faith effort to find a buyer for the property, except that a seller's agent is not required to seek additional offers to purchase the property while the property is subject to a contract for sale.

(4) A seller's agent may show properties owned by another seller to a prospective buyer and may list competing properties for sale without breaching any affirmative duty to the seller.

(5) Except as provided in subsection (3)(g) of this section, an affirmative duty may not be waived.

(6) Nothing in this section implies a duty to investigate matters that are outside the scope of the real estate licensee's expertise unless the licensee or the licensee's agent agrees in writing to investigate a matter.

696.810 Real estate licensee as buyer's agent; obligations. (1) A real estate licensee other than the seller's agent may agree with the buyer to act as the buyer's agent only. The buyer's agent is not representing the seller, even if the buyer's agent is receiving compensation for services rendered, either in full or in part, from the seller or through the seller's agent.

(2) A buyer's agent owes the buyer, other principals and the principals' agents involved in a real estate transaction the following affirmative duties:

(a) To deal honestly and in good faith;

(b) To present all written offers, written notices and other written communications to and from the parties in a timely manner without regard to whether the property is subject to a contract for sale or the buyer is already a party to a contract to purchase; and

(c) To disclose material facts known by the buyer's agent and not apparent or readily ascertainable to a party.

(3) A buyer's agent owes the buyer involved in a real estate transaction the following affirmative duties:

(a) To exercise reasonable care and diligence;

(b) To account in a timely manner for money and property received from or on behalf of the buyer;

(c) To be loyal to the buyer by not taking action that is adverse or detrimental to the buyer's interest in a transaction;

(d) To disclose in a timely manner to the buyer any conflict of interest, existing or contemplated;

(e) To advise the buyer to seek expert advice on matters related to the transaction that are beyond the agent's expertise;

(f) To maintain confidential information from or about the buyer except under subpoena or court order, even after termination of the agency relationship; and

(g) Unless agreed otherwise in writing, to make a continuous, good faith effort to find property for the buyer, except that a buyer's agent is not required to seek additional properties for the buyer while the buyer is subject to a contract for purchase or to show properties for which there is no written agreement to pay compensation to the buyer's agent.

(4) A buyer's agent may show properties in which the buyer is interested to other prospective buyers without breaching an affirmative duty to the buyer.

(5) Except as provided in subsection (3)(g) of this section, an affirmative duty may not be waived.

(6) Nothing in this section implies a duty to investigate matters that are outside the scope of the real estate licensee's expertise unless the licensee or the licensee's agent agrees in writing to investigate a matter.

696.815 Representation of both buyer and seller; obligations. (1) A real estate licensee may represent both the seller and the buyer in a real estate transaction under a disclosed limited agency agreement, with full disclosure of the relationship under the agreement.

(2) A real estate licensee acting pursuant to a disclosed limited agency agreement has the following duties and obligations:

(a) To the seller, the duties under ORS 696.805;

(b) To the buyer, the duties under ORS 696.810; and

(c) To both seller and buyer, except with express written permission of the respective person, the duty not to disclose to the other person:

(A) That the seller will accept a price lower or terms less favorable than the listing price or terms;

(B) That the buyer will pay a price greater or terms more favorable than the offering price or terms; or

(C) Specific confidential information as defined in ORS 696.800 (3).

(3) Nothing in this section implies a duty to investigate matters that are outside the scope of the real estate licensee's expertise unless the licensee agrees in writing to investigate a matter.

(4) In a real estate transaction in which different real estate brokers associated with the same principal real estate broker establish agency relationships with different parties to the real estate transaction, the principal real estate broker shall be the only broker acting as a disclosed limited agent representing both seller and buyer. Other brokers shall continue to represent only the party with whom the broker has an agency relationship unless all parties agree otherwise in writing.

(5) The principal real estate broker and the real estate licensees representing either seller or buyer shall owe the following duties to the seller and buyer:

(a) To disclose a conflict of interest in writing to all parties;

(b) To take no action that is adverse or detrimental to either party's interest in the transaction; and

(c) To obey the lawful instructions of both parties.

696.820 Agency disclosure pamphlet; rules. (1) The Real Estate Commissioner shall prescribe by rule the format and content of an initial agency disclosure pamphlet. The rules must provide that the initial agency disclosure pamphlet is informational only and may not be construed to be evidence of intent to create an agency relationship.

(2) An agent shall provide a copy of the initial agency disclosure pamphlet at the first contact with each represented party to a real property transaction, including but not limited to contacts in person, by telephone, over the Internet or the World Wide Web, or by electronic mail, electronic bulletin board or a similar electronic method.

696.822 Liability of principal for act, error or omission of agent or subagent. (1) A principal is not liable for an act, error or omission by an agent or subagent of the principal arising out of an agency relationship established under ORS 696.805, 696.810, 696.815 or 696.820:

(a) Unless the principal participates in or authorizes the act, error or omission; and

(b) Only to the extent that:

(A) The principal benefited from the act, error or omission; and

(B) A court or arbitrator determines that it is highly probable that the claimant would be unable to enforce a judgment against the agent or subagent of the principal.

(2) A real estate licensee is not liable for an act, error or omission by a principal or an agent of a principal that is not related to the licensee unless the licensee participates in or authorizes the act, error or omission. This subsection does not limit the liability of a principal real estate broker for an act, error or omission by a real estate licensee under the principal broker's supervision.

(3) Unless acknowledged by a principal in writing, facts known by an agent or subagent of the principal may not be imputed to the principal if the principal does not have actual knowledge.

(4) Unless acknowledged by a real estate licensee in writing, facts known by a principal or an agent of the principal may not be imputed to the licensee if the licensee does not have actual knowledge. This subsection does not limit the knowledge imputed to a principal real estate broker of facts known by a real estate licensee under the supervision of the principal real estate broker.

696.835 Buyer and seller responsibilities. None of the affirmative obligations of a real estate licensee or agent in a real estate transaction under ORS 696.805, 696.810 or 696.815 relieves a seller or a buyer from the responsibility to protect the seller's or buyer's own interests respectively.

696.840 Compensation and agency relationships. The payment of compensation or the obligation to pay compensation to a real estate licensee by the seller or the buyer is not necessarily determinative of a particular agency relationship between a real estate licensee and the seller or the buyer. After full disclosure of agency relationships, a listing agent, a selling agent or a real estate licensee or any combination of the three may agree to share any compensation or commission paid, or any right to any compensation or commission for which an obligation arises as the result of a real property transaction, and the terms of the agreement shall not necessarily be determinative of a particular relationship. Nothing in this section shall prevent the parties from selecting a relationship not specifically prohibited by ORS 696.301, 696.392, 696.600 to 696.785, 696.800 to 696.855 and 696.995.

696.845 Acknowledgment of existing agency relationships form. At the time of signing an offer to purchase, each buyer shall acknowledge the existing agency relationships, if any. At the time a seller accepts an offer to purchase, each seller shall acknowledge the existing agency relationships, if any. An agent to the real property transaction shall obtain the signatures of the buyers and the sellers to the acknowledgment, which shall be incorporated into or attached as an addendum to the offer to purchase or to the acceptance. The Real Estate Agency shall prescribe by rule the form and content of the acknowledgment of existing agency relationships.

696.855 Common law application to statutory obligations and remedies. (1) ORS 696.301, 696.392, 696.600 to 696.785 and 696.995 do not directly, indirectly or by implication limit or alter any preexisting common law or statutory right or remedy including actions for fraud, negligence or equitable relief.
(2) The terms "loyalty," "obedience," "disclosure," "confidentiality," "reasonable care and diligence" and "accounting in dealings" shall be interpreted under the common law of agency.
(3) Common law and statutory remedies are not affected by ORS 696.301, 696.392, 696.600 to 696.785 and 696.995.

696.870 Duties of real estate licensee under ORS 105.465 to 105.490, 696.301 and 696.870. (1)(a) A real estate licensee representing a seller of real property has a duty to inform each represented seller of the seller's duties created by this section and ORS 105.465 to 105.490 and 696.301.
(b) A real estate licensee representing a buyer of real property has a duty to inform each represented buyer of the buyer's rights under this section and ORS 105.465 to 105.490 and 696.301.
(2) If a real estate licensee performs the duties set forth in subsection (1) of this section, the real estate licensee shall have no further duties under this section.
(3) Notwithstanding subsections (1) and (2) of this section, for the purposes of ORS 696.301, a real estate licensee:
(a) Representing a seller by written agreement or course of conduct is bound by the standards of conduct and duties created under ORS 696.805;
(b) Representing a buyer by written agreement or course of conduct is bound by the standards of conduct and duties created under ORS 696.810; and
(c) Acting as a disclosed limited agent by a written agreement or course of conduct is bound by the standards of conduct and duties created under ORS 696.815.

696.880 Licensee not required to disclose proximity of registered sex offender. Nothing in ORS 181.586, 181.587, 181.588, 181.589, 696.301, 696.805, 696.810, 696.815 or 696.855 creates an obligation on the part of a person licensed under this chapter to disclose to a potential purchaser of residential property that a convicted sex offender registered under ORS 181.595, 181.596 or 181.597 resides in the area.

Note: We reproduce here ORS 105.465 to 105.490 (Seller's Property Disclosure Statements) as amended by the 2003 Legislature (Senate Bill 515). At the time of this printing (January, 2004) the Legislative Council has not yet published the final draft of these statutes, even though the bill has an effective date of January 1, 2004. To enable students to study the text of the law currently in effect we have edited these statutes according to the provisions of Senate Bill 515. When the Legislative Council publishes the final draft of the statutes the exact language may differ slightly. Students wanting the final official version of the statute should check on the internet web site of the Oregon Legislature.

SELLER'S PROPERTY DISCLOSURE STATEMENTS
105.465 Application of ORS 105.465 to 105.490, 696.301 and 696.870; form of disclosure statement.(1) The provisions of ors 105.465 to 105.490, 696.301 and 696.870:

(a) Apply to the real property described in subparagraphs (A) to (D) of this paragraph unless the buyer indicates to the seller, which indication shall be conclusive, that the buyer will use the real property for purposes other than a residence for the buyer or the buyer's spouse, parent or child:

(A) Real property consisting of or improved by one to four dwelling units;

(B) A condominium unit as defined in ors 100.005 and not subject to disclosure under ors 100.705;

(C) A timeshare property as defined in ors 94.803 and not subject to disclosure under ors 94.829; and

(D) A manufactured dwelling, as defined in ors 446.003, that is owned by the same person who owns the land upon which the manufactured dwelling is situated.

(b) Do not apply to a leasehold in real property.

(2) Except as provided in ORS 105.475 (4), a seller shall complete, sign and deliver a seller's property disclosure statement to each buyer who makes a written offer to purchase real property in this state. If required under ORS 105.465, a seller shall deliver in substantially the following form the seller's property disclosure statement to each buyer who makes a written offer to purchase real property in this state:

INSTRUCTIONS TO THE SELLER
Please complete the following form. Do not leave any spaces blank. Please refer to the line number(s) of the question(s) when you provide your explanation(s). If you are not claiming an exclusion or refusing to provide the form under ORS 105.475 (4), you should date and sign each page of this disclosure statement and each attachment.

Each seller of residential property described in ORS 105.465 must deliver this form to each buyer who makes a written offer to purchase. Under ORS 105.475 (4), refusal to provide this form gives the buyer the right to revoke their offer at any time prior to closing the transaction. Use only the section(s) of the form that apply to the transaction for which the form is used. If you are claiming an exclusion under ORS 105.470, fill out only Section 1.

An exclusion may be claimed only if the seller qualifies for the exclusion under the law. If not excluded, the seller must disclose the condition of the property or the buyer may revoke their offer to purchase anytime prior to closing the transaction. Questions regarding the legal consequences of the seller's choice should be directed to a qualified attorney.

(DO NOT FILL OUT THIS SECTION UNLESS YOU ARE CLAIMING AN EXCLUSION UNDER ORS 105.470)

Section 1. EXCLUSION FROM ORS 105.465 TO 105.490: You may claim an exclusion under ORS 105.470 only if you qualify under the statute. If you are not claiming an exclusion, you must fill out Section 2 of this form completely.

Initial only the exclusion you wish to claim.

[ ] This is the first sale of a dwelling never occupied. The dwelling is constructed or installed under building or installation permit(s) # ————— , issued by

————————————————————————.

[ ] This sale is by a financial institution that acquired the property as custodian, agent or trustee, or by foreclosure or deed in lieu of foreclosure.
[ ] The seller is a court appointed receiver, personal representative, trustee, conservator or guardian.
[ ] This sale or transfer is by a governmental agency.
Signature(s) of Seller claiming exclusion

————————————————————————
Date —————————
Buyer(s) to acknowledge Seller's claim

————————————————————————
Date —————————
(IF YOU DID NOT CLAIM AN EXCLUSION IN SECTION 1, YOU MUST FILL OUT THIS SECTION.)
Section 2. SELLER'S PROPERTY DISCLOSURE STATEMENT
(NOT A WARRANTY)
(ORS 105.465)

NOTICE TO THE BUYER: THE FOLLOWING REPRESENTATIONS ARE MADE BY THE SELLER(S) CONCERNING THE CONDITION OF THE PROPERTY LOCATED AT —————————————————— ("THE PROPERTY").

DISCLOSURES CONTAINED IN THIS FORM ARE PROVIDED BY THE SELLER ON THE BASIS OF SELLER'S ACTUAL KNOWLEDGE OF THE PROPERTY AT THE TIME OF DISCLOSURE. BUYER HAS FIVE DAYS FROM THE SELLER'S DELIVERY OF THIS SELLER'S DISCLOSURE STATEMENT TO REVOKE BUYER'S OFFER BY DELIVERING BUYER'S SEPARATE SIGNED WRITTEN STATEMENT OF REVOCATION TO THE SELLER DISAPPROVING THE SELLER'S DISCLOSURE STATEMENT, UNLESS BUYER WAIVES THIS RIGHT AT OR PRIOR TO ENTERING INTO A SALE AGREEMENT.

FOR A MORE COMPREHENSIVE EXAMINATION OF THE SPECIFIC CONDITION OF THIS PROPERTY, BUYER IS ADVISED TO OBTAIN AND PAY FOR THE SERVICES OF A QUALIFIED SPECIALIST TO INSPECT THE PROPERTY ON BUYER'S BEHALF INCLUDING, FOR EXAMPLE, ONE OR MORE OF THE FOLLOWING: ARCHITECTS, ENGINEERS, PLUMBERS, ELECTRICIANS, ROOFERS, ENVIRONMENTAL INSPECTORS, BUILDING INSPECTORS, CERTIFIED HOME INSPECTORS, OR PEST AND DRY ROT INSPECTORS.

Seller is/ is not occupying the property.

I. SELLER'S REPRESENTATIONS:

The following are representations made by the seller and are not the representations of any financial institution that may have made or may make a loan pertaining to the property, or that may have or take a security interest in the property, or any real estate licensee engaged by the seller or the buyer.

*If you mark yes on items with *, attach a copy or explain on an attached sheet.

1. TITLE

A. Do you have legal authority to sell the property? [ ] Yes [ ] No [ ] Unknown

*B. Is title to the property subject to any of the following: [ ] Yes [ ] No [ ] Unknown

(1) First right of refusal

(2) Option

(3) Lease or rental agreement

(4) Other listing

(5) Life estate?

*C. Are there any encroachments, boundary agreements, boundary disputes or recent boundary changes? [ ] Yes [ ] No [ ] Unknown

*D. Are there any rights of way, easements, licenses, access limitations or claims that may affect your interest in the property? [ ] Yes [ ] No [ ] Unknown

*E. Are there any agreements for joint maintenance of an easement or right of way? [ ] Yes [ ] No [ ] Unknown

*F. Are there any governmental studies, designations, zoning overlays, surveys or notices that would affect the property? [ ] Yes [ ] No [ ] Unknown

*G. Are there any pending or existing governmental assessments against the property? [ ] Yes [ ] No [ ] Unknown

*H. Are there any zoning violations or nonconforming uses? [ ] Yes [ ] No [ ] Unknown

*I. Is there a boundary survey for the property? [ ] Yes [ ] No [ ] Unknown

*J. Are there any covenants, conditions, restrictions or private assessments that affect the property? [ ] Yes [ ] No [ ] Unknown

*K. Is the property subject to any special tax assessment or tax treatment that may result in levy of additional taxes if the property is sold? [ ] Yes [ ] No [ ] Unknown

2. WATER

A. Household water

(1) The source of the water is (check ALL that apply): [ ] Public [ ] Community [ ] Private [ ] Other

(2) Water source information:

*a. Does the water source require a water permit? [ ] Yes [ ] No [ ] Unknown

If yes, do you have a permit? [ ] YES [ ] NO

b. Is the water source located on the property? [ ] Yes [ ] No [ ] Unknown

*If not, are there any written agreements for a shared water source? [ ] Yes [ ] No [ ] Unknown [ ] NA

*c. Is there an easement (recorded or unrecorded) for your access to or maintenance of the water source? [ ] Yes [ ] No [ ] Unknown

d. If the source of water is from a well or spring, have you had any of the following in the past 12 months? [ ] Flow test [ ] Bacteria test [ ] Chemical contents test [ ] Yes [ ] No [ ] Unknown [ ] NA

*e. Are there any water source plumbing problems or needed repairs? [ ] Yes [ ] No [ ] Unknown

(3) Are there any water treatment systems for the property? [ ] Yes [ ] No [ ] Unknown [ ] Leased [ ] Owned

B. Irrigation

(1) Are there any [ ] water rights or [ ] other irrigation rights for the property? [ ] Yes [ ] No [ ] Unknown

*(2) If any exist, has the irrigation water been used during the last five-year period? [ ] Yes [ ] No

[ ] Unknown [ ] NA

*(3) Is there a water rights certificate or other written evidence available? [ ] Yes [ ] No [ ] Unknown [ ] NA

C. Outdoor sprinkler system

(1) Is there an outdoor sprinkler system for the property? [ ] Yes [ ] No [ ] Unknown

(2) Has a back flow valve been installed? [ ] Yes [ ] No [ ] Unknown [ ] NA

(3) Is the outdoor sprinkler system operable? [ ] Yes [ ] No [ ] Unknown [ ] NA

3. SEWAGE SYSTEM

A. Is the property connected to a public or community sewage system? [ ] Yes [ ] No [ ] Unknown

B. Are there any new public or community sewage systems proposed for the property? [ ] Yes [ ] No [ ] Unknown

C. Is the property connected to an on-site septic system? [ ] Yes [ ] No [ ] Unknown

If yes, was it installed by permit? [ ] Yes [ ] No [ ] Unknown [ ] NA

*Has the system been repaired or altered? [ ] Yes [ ] No [ ] Unknown

Has the condition of the system been evaluated and a report issued? [ ] Yes [ ] No [ ] Unknown

Has it ever been pumped? [ ] Yes [ ] No [ ] Unknown [ ] NA

If yes, when? —————————————

*D. Are there any sewage system problems or needed repairs? [ ] Yes [ ] No [ ] Unknown

E. Does your sewage system require on-site pumping to another level? [ ] Yes [ ] No [ ] Unknown

4. DWELLING INSULATION

A. Is there insulation in the:

(1) Ceiling? [ ] Yes [ ] No [ ] Unknown

(2) Exterior walls? [ ] Yes [ ] No [ ] Unknown

(3) Floors? [ ] Yes [ ] No [ ] Unknown

B. Are there any defective insulated doors or windows? [ ] Yes [ ] No [ ] Unknown

5. DWELLING STRUCTURE

*A. Has the roof leaked? [ ] Yes [ ] No [ ] Unknown

If yes, has it been repaired? [ ] Yes [ ] No [ ] Unknown [ ] NA

B. Are there any additions, conversions or remodeling? [ ] Yes [ ] No [ ] Unknown

If yes, was a building permit required? [ ] Yes [ ] No [ ] Unknown [ ] NA

If yes, was a building permit obtained? [ ] Yes [ ] No [ ] Unknown [ ] NA

If yes, was final inspection obtained? [ ] Yes [ ] No [ ] Unknown [ ] NA

C. Are there smoke alarms or detectors? [ ] Yes [ ] No [ ] Unknown

D. Is there a woodstove included in the sale? [ ] Yes [ ] No [ ] Unknown

Make —————————————

*E. Has pest and dry rot, structural or "whole house" inspection been done within the last three years? [ ] Yes [ ] No [ ] Unknown

*F. Are there any moisture problems, areas of water penetration, mildew odors or other moisture conditions (especially in the basement)? [ ] Yes [ ] No [ ] Unknown

*If yes, explain on attached sheet the frequency and extent of problem and any insurance claims, repairs or remediation done.

G. Is there a sump pump on the property? [ ] Yes [ ] No [ ] Unknown

H. Are there any materials used in the construction of the structure that are or have been the subject of a recall, class action suit, settlement or litigation? [ ] Yes [ ] No [ ] Unknown

If yes, what are the materials? —————————————

(1) Are there problems with the materials? [ ] Yes [ ] No [ ] Unknown [ ] NA

(2) Are the materials covered by a warranty? [ ] Yes [ ] No [ ] Unknown [ ] NA

(3) Have the materials been inspected? [ ] Yes [ ] No [ ] Unknown [ ] NA

(4) Have there ever been claims filed for these materials by you or by previous owners? [ ] Yes [ ] No [ ] Unknown [ ] NA

If yes, when? —————————————

(5) Was money received? [ ] Yes [ ] No [ ] Unknown [ ] NA

(6) Were any of the materials repaired or replaced? [ ] Yes [ ] No [ ] Unknown [ ] NA

6. DWELLING SYSTEMS AND FIXTURES

If the following systems or fixtures are included in the purchase price, are they in good working order on the date this form is signed?

A. Electrical system, including wiring, switches, outlets and service [ ] Yes [ ] No [ ] Unknown

B. Plumbing system, including pipes, faucets, fixtures and toilets [ ] Yes [ ] No [ ] Unknown

C. Water heater tank [ ] Yes [ ] No [ ] Unknown

D. Garbage disposal [ ] Yes [ ] No [ ] Unknown [ ] NA

E. Built-in range and oven [ ] Yes [ ] No [ ] Unknown [ ] NA

F. Built-in dishwasher [ ] Yes [ ] No [ ] Unknown [ ] NA

G. Sump pump [ ] Yes [ ] No [ ] Unknown [ ] NA
H. Heating and cooling systems [ ] Yes [ ] No [ ] Unknown [ ] NA
I. Security system [ ] Owned [ ] Leased [ ] Yes [ ] No [ ] Unknown [ ] NA
J. Are there any materials or products used in the systems and fixtures that are or have been the subject of a recall, class action settlement or other litigations? [ ] Yes [ ] No [ ] Unknown
If yes, what product? ——————————
(1) Are there problems with the product? [ ] Yes [ ] No [ ] Unknown
(2) Is the product covered by a warranty? [ ] Yes [ ] No [ ] Unknown
(3) Has the product been inspected? [ ] Yes [ ] No [ ] Unknown
(4) Have claims been filed for this product by you or by previous owners? [ ] Yes [ ] No [ ] Unknown
If yes, when? ——————————
(5) Was money received? [ ] Yes [ ] No [ ] Unknown
(6) Were any of the materials or products repaired or replaced? [ ] Yes [ ] No [ ] Unknown

7. COMMON INTEREST
A. Is there a Home Owners' Association or other governing entity? [ ] Yes [ ] No [ ] Unknown
Name of Association or Other Governing Entity

——————————————————————

Contact Person ——————————————
Address ———————————————————
Phone Number ————————————————
B. Regular periodic assessments: $ ——————
per [ ] Month [ ] Year [ ] Other
*C. Are there any pending or proposed special assessments? [ ] Yes [ ] No [ ] Unknown
D. Are there shared "common areas" or joint maintenance agreements for facilities like walls, fences, pools, tennis courts, walkways or other areas co-owned in undivided interest with others? [ ] Yes [ ] No [ ] Unknown
E. Is the Home Owners' Association or other governing entity a party to pending litigation or subject to an unsatisfied judgment? [ ] Yes [ ] No [ ] Unknown [ ] NA
F. Is the property in violation of recorded covenants, conditions and restrictions or in violation of other bylaws or governing rules, whether recorded or not? [ ] Yes [ ] No [ ] Unknown [ ] NA

8. GENERAL
A. Are there problems with settling, soil, standing water or drainage on the property or in the immediate area? [ ] Yes [ ] No [ ] Unknown

B. Does the property contain fill? [ ] Yes [ ] No [ ] Unknown
C. Is there any material damage to the property or any of the structure(s) from fire, wind, floods, beach movements, earthquake, expansive soils or landslides? [ ] Yes [ ] No [ ] Unknown
D. Is the property in a designated floodplain? [ ] Yes [ ] No [ ] Unknown
E. Is the property in a designated slide or other geologic hazard zone? [ ] Yes [ ] No [ ] Unknown
*F. Has any portion of the property been tested or treated for asbestos, formaldehyde, radon gas, lead-based paint, mold, fuel or chemical storage tanks or contaminated soil or water? [ ] Yes [ ] No [ ] Unknown
G. Are there any tanks or underground storage tanks (e.g., septic, chemical, fuel, etc.) on the property? [ ] Yes [ ] No [ ] Unknown
H. Has the property ever been used as an illegal drug manufacturing or distribution site? [ ] Yes [ ] No [ ] Unknown
*If yes, was a Certificate of Fitness issued? [ ] Yes [ ] No [ ] Unknown

9. FULL DISCLOSURE BY SELLERS
*A. Are there any other material defects affecting this property or its value that a prospective buyer should know about? [ ] Yes [ ] No
*If yes, describe the defect on attached sheet and explain the frequency and extent of the problem and any insurance claims, repairs or remediation.
B. Verification:
The foregoing answers and attached explanations (if any) are complete and correct to the best of my/our knowledge and I/we have received a copy of this disclosure statement. I/we authorize my/our agents to deliver a copy of this disclosure statement to all prospective buyers of the property or their agents.
SELLER(S) SIGNATURE: ———————————
SELLER DATE ——————————
SELLER DATE ——————————

11. Buyer's Acknowledgment
A. As buyer(s), I/we acknowledge the duty to pay diligent attention to any material defects that are known to me/us or can be known by me/us by utilizing diligent attention and observation.
B. Each buyer acknowledges and understands that the disclosures set forth in this statement and in any amendments to this statement are made only by the seller and are not the representations of any financial institution that may have made or may make a loan pertaining to the property, or that may have or take a

security interest in the property, or of any real estate licensee engaged by the seller or buyer. A financial institution or real estate licensee is not bound by and has no liability with respect to any representation, misrepresentation, omission, error or inaccuracy contained in another party's disclosure statement required by this section or any amendment to the disclosure statement.

C. Buyer (which term includes all persons signing the "buyer's acknowledgment" portion of this disclosure statement below) hereby acknowledges receipt of a copy of this disclosure statement (including attachments, if any) bearing seller's signature(s). DISCLOSURES, IF ANY, CONTAINED IN THIS FORM ARE PROVIDED BY THE SELLER ON THE BASIS OF SELLER'S ACTUAL KNOWLEDGE OF THE PROPERTY AT THE TIME OF DISCLOSURE. IF THE SELLER HAS FILLED OUT SECTION 2 OF THIS FORM, YOU, THE BUYER, HAVE FIVE DAYS FROM THE SELLER'S DELIVERY OF THIS DISCLOSURE STATEMENT TO REVOKE YOUR OFFER BY DELIVERING YOUR SEPARATE SIGNED WRITTEN STATEMENT OF REVOCATION TO THE SELLER DISAPPROVING THE SELLER'S DISCLOSURE UNLESS YOU WAIVE THIS RIGHT AT OR PRIOR TO ENTERING INTO A SALE AGREEMENT.

BUYER HEREBY ACKNOWLEDGES RECEIPT OF A COPY OF THIS SELLER'S PROPERTY DISCLOSURE STATEMENT.

Buyer ——————————————————
Date ————————————
Buyer ——————————————————
Date ————————————
Agent receiving disclosure statement on buyer's behalf to sign and date:
Real Estate Licensee ——————————————
Real Estate Firm ——————————————————
Date received by agent ————————————

————————————————————————

(3) "Financial institution" has the meaning given that term in ORS 706.008. "Financial institution" includes mortgage bankers and mortgage brokers, as those terms are defined in ORS 59.840, and consumer finance companies licensed under ORS chapter 725.

(4) "Real estate licensee" has the meaning given that term in ORS 696.010.

105.470 Exclusions from ORS 105.465 to 105.490. ORS 105.465 to 105.490, 696.301 and 696.870 do not apply to:

(1) The first sale of a dwelling never occupied, provided that the seller provides the buyer with the following statement on or before the date the buyer is legally obligated to purchase the subject real property: "THIS HOME WAS CONSTRUCTED OR INSTALLED UNDER BUILDING OR INSTALLATION PERMIT(S) # ——————————, ISSUED BY ——————————"

(2) Sales by financial institutions that acquired the property as custodian, agent or trustee, or by foreclosure or deed in lieu of foreclosure.

(3) The following sellers, if appointed by a court:

(a) Receivers;

(b) Personal representatives;

(c) Trustees;

(d) Conservators; or

(e) Guardians.

(4) Sales or transfers by governmental agencies.

105.475 Revocation of offer; criteria. (1) If a seller issues a seller's property disclosure statement and a buyer has not then delivered to the seller a written statement waiving the buyer's right to revoke the buyer's offer, the buyer shall have five business days after delivery of the seller's property disclosure statement to revoke the buyer's offer by delivering to the seller a separate signed written statement of revocation disapproving the seller's disclosure.

(2) If a buyer fails to timely deliver to a seller a written statement revoking the buyer's offer, the buyer's right to revoke the buyer's offer expires.

(3) If a buyer closes the transaction, the buyer's right to revoke based on ORS 105.465 to 105.490, 696.301 and 696.870 is terminated.

(4) If the seller fails or refuses to provide a seller's property disclosure statement as required under this section, the buyer shall have a right of revocation until the right is terminated pursuant to subsection (3) of this section.

(5) If the buyer revokes the offer pursuant to this section, notwithstanding ORS 696.581, the buyer is entitled to immediate return of all deposits and other considerations delivered to any party or escrow agent with respect to the buyer's offer, and the buyer's offer is void.

(6) When the deposits and other considerations have been returned to the buyer, upon the buyer's signed, written release and indemnification of the holders of the deposits and other considerations, the holders are released from all liability for the deposits and other considerations.

(7) Any seller's property disclosure statement issued by the seller is part of and incorporated into the offer and the acceptance.

105.480 Representations in disclosure statement; application. (1) The representations contained in a seller's property disclosure statement and in any amendment to the disclosure statement are the representations of the seller only. The representations of the seller are not representations of:

(a) A financial institution that may have made or that may make a loan pertaining to the property covered by a seller's property disclosure statement, or that may have or take a security interest in the property covered by a seller's property disclosure statement.

(b) A real estate licensee engaged by the seller or buyer.

(2) Neither a financial institution nor a real estate licensee is bound by or has any liability with respect to any representation, misrepresentation, omission, error or inaccuracy contained in the seller's property disclosure statement required by ORS 105.465 or any amendment to the disclosure statement.

105.485 Allocation of burden of proof. The burden of proof of lawful delivery of a seller's property disclosure statement and any amendment thereto is on the seller. The burden of proof of lawful delivery of a notice of revocation of a buyer's offer is on the buyer.

105.490 Effect of ors 105.465 to 105.490 on rights and remedies. ORS 105.465 to 105.490, 696.301 and 696.870 do not directly, indirectly or by implication limit or alter any preexisting common law or statutory right or remedy including actions for fraud, negligence or equitable relief.

ADMINISTRATIVE RULES
REGARDING AGENCY

Agency Relationships

863-015-0200 (1) Unless the parties expressly agree to a different relationship not otherwise prohibited by law, the types of agency relationships a real estate licensee may establish in a real estate transaction are limited to the following:

(a) An agency relationship between a real estate licensee and the seller exclusively;

(b) An agency relationship between a real estate licensee and the buyer exclusively;

(c) A disclosed limited agency relationship where one or more real estate licensees associated with the same principal broker represent both the seller and the buyer in the same real estate transaction;

(d) A disclosed limited agency relationship where real estate licensees associated with the same principal broker are designated to represent, respectively, the buyer exclusively and the seller exclusively;

(e) A disclosed limited agency relationship where one or more real estate licensees associated with the same principal broker represent more than one buyer in the same real estate transaction.

(2) Unless the parties expressly agree to a different relationship not otherwise prohibited by law:

(a) A licensee representing a seller by written agreement or course of conduct establishes an agency relationship under sections (1)(a) or (d) above;

(b) A licensee representing a buyer by written agreement or course of conduct establishes an agency relationship under sections (1)(b) or (d) above;

(c) A licensee representing both a buyer and a seller or two or more buyers in the same real estate transaction is a disclosed limited agent of both the buyer and seller or all buyers under sections (1)(c) or (e) above,.

(3) When an agency relationship is formed between a real estate licensee and a client under section (2) above, the following apply:

(a) The principal broker with whom the licensee is associated is the agent of the client;

(b) In a real estate transaction in which different real estate licensees associated with the same principal broker establish agency relationships with different parties to the real estate transaction, the principal broker shall be the only disclosed limited agent of both parties.

(c) In a real estate transaction in which one or more real estate licensees associated with the same principal broker establish agency relationships with more than one party to the real estate transaction, those licensees and the principal broker shall be the only disclosed limited agents of those parties.

(4) Except as provided in sections (2) and (3) above, licensees affiliated with the same real estate business are not agents of all clients of the real estate business.

(5) Payment, or promise of payment, of a real estate commission or other fee does not by itself create an agency relationship.

(6) A principal real estate broker acting as a disclosed limited agent under section (3)(b) above, shall do each of the following:

(a) Supervise the licensees associated with the principal broker in fulfillment of their duties and obligations to their respective clients;

(b) Avoid advocating on behalf of either the seller or the buyer; and

(c) Avoid disclosing or utilizing, without permission, confidential information of any client with whom the principal broker has an agency relationship.

(7) Real estate licensees associated with a principal broker who is acting as a disclosed limited agent under section (3)(b) above, shall do both of the following:

(a) Serve as the agent of only the party or parties in the transaction with whom the real estate licensee has established an agency relationship; and

(b) Fulfill the duties owed to the respective client as set forth in the ORS 696.815 and as agreed in a disclosed limited agency agreement entered into pursuant to OAR 863-015-0210.

(8) All real estate licensees associated with a principal broker who are acting as disclosed limited agents under section (2)(c) above, shall refrain from disclosing or utilizing any confidential information relating to the other party that has been acquired as a result of the licensee's association with the principal broker, unless authorized to do so by that party.

(9) Nothing in this rule prohibits licensees from disclosing or utilizing factual, non-confidential information relating to all parties to a transaction in order to fulfill a licensee's duties to the client under ORS 696.815.

(10) If a principal real estate broker acting as a disclosed limited agent under section (3)(b) above, determines that confidential information of one principal to a transaction has become known to another

client in the transaction as the result of a violation of sections (6)(c) or (7)(b) above, the principal broker shall promptly and fully disclose the violation to the affected client in writing.

(11) Affirmative duties under ORS 696.805 and 696.810, where appropriate, apply to the agents, principal, other principals and the principals' agents but do not create fiduciary, or other similar, duties inconsistent with the actual legal relationship between an agent and other principals to a transaction or that principals' agents.

(12)(a) The Final Agency Acknowledgement of the agency relationships described in this section and required by ORS 696.845 shall be printed in substantially the following form:

FINAL AGENCY ACKNOWLEDGEMENT

Both Buyer and Seller acknowledge having received the Oregon Real Estate Agency Disclosure Pamphlet, and hereby acknowledge and consent to the following agency relationships in this transaction:

(1) _____ (Name of Selling Licensee) of _____ (Name of Real Estate Firm) is the agent of (check one) [ ] The Buyer exclusively. [ ] The Seller exclusively (Seller Agency"). [ ] Both the Buyer and the Seller ("Disclosed Limited Agency").

(2) _____ (Name of Listing Licensee) of _____ (Name of Real Estate Firm) is the agent of (check one) [ ] The Seller exclusively. [ ] Both the Buyer and the Seller ("Disclosed Limited Agency").

(3) If both parties are each represented by one or more licensees in the same real estate firm, and the licensees are supervised by the same principal broker in that real estate firm, Buyer and Seller acknowledge that said principal broker shall become the disclosed limited agent for both Buyer and Seller as more fully explained in the disclosed Limited Agency Agreements that have been reviewed and signed by Buyer, Seller and Licensee(s).

Buyer shall sign this acknowledgment at the time of signing this Agreement before submission to Seller. Seller shall sign this acknowledgment at the time this Agreement is first submitted to Seller, even if this Agreement will be rejected or a counter offer will be made. Sellers signature to this Final Agency Acknowledgment shall not constitute acceptance of the Agreement or any terms therein.

ACKNOWLEDGED

Buyer: _____ Print _____ Dated: _____

Buyer: _____ Print _____ Dated: _____

Seller: _____ Print _____ Dated: _____

Seller: _____ Print _____ Dated: _____

(b) If incorporated as a part of a preprinted agreement, the Final Agency Acknowledgement required by subsection (a) shall appear at the top of the first page of the preprinted agreement, separate and apart from the sale agreement and shall be signed separately from the sale agreement. If the Final Agency Acknowledgement required by subsection (b) is not included within a preprinted agreement, the Final Agency Acknowledgement shall also include the property address or legal description of the subject property, a reference to the attached sale agreement, and shall include separate signature lines for buyers and sellers.

(Note: OAR 200 (12) was added January 1, 2004.)

Disclosed Limited Agency

863-015-0205 (1) Licensees shall establish the agency relationships described in OAR 863-015-0200(1)(c) to (e) only by written agreement. Such agreements shall meet all the requirements of OAR 863-015-0210.

(2) A disclosed limited agency relationship shall exist when a single licensee undertakes by written agreement or conduct to represent more than one party to a real estate transaction. For the purpose of this rule, two or more buyers shall be considered involved in the same real estate transaction when all have submitted offers on the same real property.

(3) Except as provided for in section (5), a disclosed limited agency relationship shall exist when two or more licensees supervised by the same principal broker undertake by written agreement or conduct to represent more than one party to a real estate transaction. Notwithstanding the other provisions of this rule, individual agents may be designated to represent the buyer exclusively or the seller exclusively as described in OAR 863-015- 0200(1)(c), (d) and (e).

(4) The following conditions shall apply to the agency relationship described in OAR 863-015-0200(1)(c), (d) and (e):

(a) The principal broker with whom the licensee is associated shall have a written policy as required by OAR 863- 015-0220 and established procedures to assure that a licensee who represents one client will not have access to and will not obtain confidential information concerning another client involved in the same transaction;

(b) In situations where a real estate business has two or more principal brokers, each principal broker shall be the disclosed limited agent of all clients in the transaction unless each of the following conditions are met:

(A) The principal brokers have entered into a written agreement and have written office policies dividing control and supervision responsibilities and have individually complied with subsection (a) above. Principal brokers may comply with subsection (a) above by holding open records of real estate activity in different offices or by otherwise initiating procedures that secure open records in such a way as to prevent licensees representing different parties to the same transaction from accessing or obtaining confidential information concerning another party to the transaction;

(B) The licensees designated to represent the seller exclusively and the buyer exclusively are associated with the same principal broker. If the principal broker has an existing agency relationship with one party to the transaction (either as a seller's agent or buyer's agent), the principal broker, pursuant to the requirements of OAR 863-015- 0210, shall act as the disclosed limited agent of both parties and another licensee shall be designated to represent the other party exclusively.

(C) Each client to the transaction has signed a disclosed limited agency agreement that indicates which principal broker will act as the disclosed limited agent in the transaction.

(5) If principal brokers have entered into a written agreement and have written office policies dividing control and supervision responsibilities and have individually complied with subsection (4)(a) above by holding open records of real estate activity in different offices or by otherwise initiating procedures that secure open records in such a way as to prevent licensees representing different parties to the same transaction from accessing or obtaining confidential information concerning another principal in the transaction, then a transaction involving agents associated with different principal brokers is not a disclosed limited agency transaction.

Disclosed Limited Agency Agreement

863-015-0210 (1) Disclosed limited agency agreements required by ORS 696.815 shall be in writing, signed and dated by the parties to be bound or by their duly appointed real estate agents.

(2) Each disclosed limited agency agreement shall contain the following:

(a) The name of the real estate business within which the representation will take place;

(b) Identification of any existing listing or service agreement between the parties to the disclosed limited agency agreement;

(c) The name(s) of the licensee(s), including the principal real estate broker, who will represent the client;

(d) A plain language description of the requirements of ORS 696.815;

(e) Full disclosure of the duties and responsibilities of an agent who represents more than one party to a real estate transaction. This requirement can be met by providing the client with a copy of the initial agency disclosure pamphlet required by ORS 696.820, discussing the portion of the pamphlet entitled "Duties and Responsibilities of an Agent Who Represents More that One Party to a Transaction" with the client and incorporating the pamphlet into the disclosed limited agency agreement by reference;

(f) Consent and agreement between the parties to the disclosed limited agency agreement regarding representation of the client in future transactions.

(3) Use of a disclosed limited agency agreement for sellers in substantially the following form shall be deemed prima facie evidence of compliance with OAR 863-015-0210(1) and (2):

Property Address _____

Addendum to Listing Agreement Dated_____

Real Estate Firm _____

DISCLOSED LIMITED AGENCY AGREEMENT FOR SELLER

The Parties to this Disclosed Limited Agency Agreement are:

Listing Agent (print) _____

Listing Agent's Principal Broker (print)

_____

Seller (print) _____

Seller (print) _____

The Parties to this Agreement understand that Oregon law allows a single real estate agent to act as a disclosed limited agent -- to represent both the seller and the buyer in the same real estate transaction, or multiple buyers who want to purchase the same property. It is also understood that when different agents associated with the same principal broker (the broker who directly supervises the other agents) establish agency relationships with the buyer and seller in a real estate transaction, the agents' principal broker shall be the only broker acting as a disclosed limited agent representing both seller and buyer. The other agents shall continue to represent only the party with whom they have an established agency relationship, unless all parties agree otherwise in writing. In consideration of the above understanding, and the mutual promises and benefits exchanged here and in the Listing Agreement, the Parties now agree as follows:

1. Seller acknowledge they have received the initial agency disclosure pamphlet required by ORS 696.820 and have read and discussed with the Listing Agent that part of the pamphlet entitled "Duties and Responsibilities of an Agent Who Represents More than One Party to A Transaction." The initial agency disclosure pamphlet is hereby incorporated into this Disclosed Limited Agency Agreement by reference.

2. Seller, having discussed with the Listing Agent the duties and responsibilities of an agent who represents more than one party to a transaction, consent and agree as follows:

(A) The Listing Agent and the Listing Agent's Principal Broker, in addition to representing Seller, may represent one or more buyers in a transaction involving the listed property;

(B) In a transaction involving the listed property where the buyer is represented by an agent who works in the same real estate business as the Listing Agent and who is supervised by the Listing Agent's Principal Broker, the Principal Broker may represent both Seller and Buyer. In such a situation, the Listing Agent will continue to represent only the Seller and the other agent will represent only the Buyer, consistent with the applicable duties and responsibilities as set out in the initial agency disclosure pamphlet; and

(C) In all other cases, the Listing Agent and the Listing Agent's Principal Broker shall represent Seller exclusively.

Seller signature _____

Date _____

Seller signature _____

Date _____

Listing Agent signature _____

Date _____

(On their own and on behalf of Principal Broker)

Broker initial and review date_____

(4) Use of a disclosed limited agency agreement for buyers in substantially the following form shall be deemed prima facie evidence of compliance with sections (1) and (2).

Property Address _____

Addendum to Buyer Service Agreement Dated

_____

Real Estate Firm _____

Disclosed Limited Agency Agreement For Buyer

The Parties to this Disclosed Limited Agency Agreement are:

Buyer's Agent (print) _____

Buyer's Agent's Principal Broker (print)

_____

Buyer (print) _____

Buyer (print)_____

The Parties to this Agreement understand that Oregon law allows a single real estate agent to act as a disclosed limited agent -- to represent both the seller and the buyer in the same real estate transaction, or multiple buyers who want to purchase the same property. It is also understood that when different agents associated with the same principal broker (the broker who directly supervises the other agents) establish agency relationships with the buyer and seller in a real estate transaction, the agents' principal broker shall be the only broker acting as a disclosed limited agent representing both seller and buyer. The other agents shall continue to represent only the party with whom they have an established agency relationship, unless all parties agree otherwise in writing. In consideration of the above understanding, and the mutual promises and benefits exchanged here and, if applicable, in the Buyer Service Agreement, the Parties now agree as follows:

1. Buyer(s) acknowledge they have received the initial agency disclosure pamphlet required by ORS 696.820 and have read and discussed with the Buyers Agent that part of the pamphlet entitled "Duties and Responsibilities of an Agent Who Represents More than One Party to A Transaction." The initial agency disclosure pamphlet is hereby incorporated into this Disclosed Limited Agency Agreement by reference.

2. Buyer(s), having discussed with Buyers Agent the duties and responsibilities of an agent who represents more than one party to a transaction, consent and agree as follows:

(A) Buyers Agent and the Buyers Agent's Principal Broker, in addition to representing Buyer, may represent the seller or another buyer in any transaction involving Buyer;

(B) In a transaction where the seller is represented by an agent who works in the same real estate business as the Buyers Agent and who is supervised by the Buyers Agent's Principal Broker, the Principal Broker may represent both seller and Buyer. In such a situation, the Buyers Agent will continue to represent only the Buyer and the other agent will represent only the Seller, consistent with the applicable duties and responsibilities set out in the initial agency disclosure pamphlet;

(C) In all other cases, the Buyers Agent and the Buyers Agent's Principal Broker shall represent Buyer exclusively.

Buyer signature _____

Date _____

Buyer signature _____

Date _____

Buyer's Agent signature_____

Date _____

(On their own and on behalf of Principal Broker)

Broker initial and review date _____

Initial Agency Disclosure Pamphlet

863-015-0215 (1) An agent shall provide a copy of the Initial Agency Disclosure Pamphlet provided for in section (4) of this rule at first contact with each represented party to a real property transaction, including but not limited to contacts in- person, by telephone, over the Internet or World Wide Web, or by electronic mail, electronic bulletin board or a similar electronic method.

(2) An agent need not provide a copy of the Initial Agency Disclosure Pamphlet to a party who has, or may be reasonably assumed to have, already received a copy of the pamphlet from another agent.

(3) "First contact with a represented party" means contact with a person who is represented by a real estate licensee or can reasonably be assumed from the circumstances to be represented or seeking representation.

(4) The Initial Agency Disclosure Pamphlet shall be printed in substantially the following form:

OREGON REAL ESTATE AGENCY DISCLOSURE PAMPHLET
(OAR 863-015-215(4))

This pamphlet describes agency relationships and the duties and responsibilities of real estate licensees in Oregon. This pamphlet is informational only and neither the pamphlet nor its delivery to you may be construed to be evidence of intent to create an agency relationship.

Real Estate Agency Relationships

An "agency" relationship is a voluntary legal relationship in which a real estate licensee (the "agent") agrees to act on behalf of a buyer or a seller (the "client") in a real estate transaction. Oregon law provides for three types of agency relationships between real estate agents and their clients:

Seller's Agent – Represents the seller only;
Buyer's Agent – Represents the buyer only;
Disclosed Limited Agent – Represents both the buyer and seller, or multiple buyers who want to purchase the same property. This can be done only with the written permission of both clients.

The actual agency relationships between the seller, buyer and their agents in a real estate transaction must be acknowledged at the time an offer to purchase is made. Please read this pamphlet carefully before entering into an agency relationship with a real estate agent.

Duties and Responsibilities of an Agent Who Represents Only the Seller or Only the Buyer

Under a written listing agreement to sell property, an agent represents only the seller unless the seller agrees in writing to allow the agent to also represent the buyer. An agent who agrees to represent a buyer acts only as the buyer's agent unless the buyer agrees in writing to allow the agent to also represent the seller. An agent who represents only the seller or only the buyer owes the following affirmative duties to their client, other parties and their agents involved in a real estate transaction:

1. To exercise reasonable care and diligence;
2. To deal honestly and in good faith;
3. To present all written offers, notices and other communications in a timely manner whether or not the seller's property is subject to a contract for sale or the buyer is already a party to a contract to purchase;
4. To disclose material facts known by the agent and not apparent or readily ascertainable to a party;
5. To account in a timely manner for money and property received from or on behalf of the client;
6. To be loyal to their client by not taking action that is adverse or detrimental to the client's interest in a transaction;
7. To disclose in a timely manner to the client any conflict of interest, existing or contemplated;
8. To advise the client to seek expert advice on matters related to the transactions that are beyond the agent's expertise;
9. To maintain confidential information from or about the client except under subpoena or court order, even after termination of the agency relationship; and
10. When representing a seller, to make a continuous, good faith effort to find a buyer for the property, except that a seller's agent is not required to seek additional offers to purchase the property while the property is subject to a contract for sale. When representing a buyer, to make a continuous, good faith

effort to find property for the buyer, except that a buyer's agent is not required to seek additional properties for the buyer while the buyer is subject to a contract for purchase or to show properties for which there is no written agreement to pay compensation to the buyer's agent.

None of these affirmative duties of an agent may be waived, except #10, which can only be waived by written agreement between client and agent.

Under Oregon law, a seller's agent may show properties owned by another seller to a prospective buyer and may list competing properties for sale without breaching any affirmative duty to the seller. Similarly, a buyer's agent may show properties in which the buyer is interested to other prospective buyers without breaching any affirmative duty to the buyer. Unless agreed to in writing, an agent has no duty to investigate matters that are outside the scope of the agent's expertise.

Duties and Responsibilities of an Agent Who Represents More than One Client in a Transaction

One agent may represent both the seller and the buyer in the same transaction, or multiple buyers who want to purchase the same property only under a written "Disclosed Limited Agency" agreement, signed by the seller, buyer(s) and their agent.

When different agents associated with the same real estate firm establish agency relationships with different parties to the same transaction, only the principal broker (the broker who supervises the other agents) will act as a Disclosed Limited Agent for both the buyer and seller. The other agents continue to represent only the party with whom the agent already has an established agency relationship unless all parties agree otherwise in writing. The supervising principal broker and the agents representing either the seller or the buyer have the following duties to their clients:

1. To disclose a conflict of interest in writing to all parties;
2. To take no action that is adverse or detrimental to either party's interest in the transaction; and
3. To obey the lawful instruction of both parties.

An agent acting under a Disclosed Limited Agency agreement has the same duties to the client as when representing only a seller or only a buyer, except that the agent may not, without written permission, disclose any of the following:

1. That the seller will accept a lower price or less favorable terms than the listing price or terms;

2. That the buyer will pay a greater price or more favorable terms than the offering price or terms; or
3. In transactions involving one-to-four residential units only, information regarding the real property transaction including, but not limited to, price, terms, financial qualifications or motivation to buy or sell.

No matter whom they represent, an agent **must** disclose information the agent knows or should know that failure to disclose would constitute fraudulent misrepresentation. Unless agreed to in writing, an agent acting under a Disclosed Limited Agency agreement has no duty to investigate matters that are outside the scope of the agent's expertise.

You are encouraged to discuss the above information with the agent delivering this pamphlet to you. If you intend for that agent, or any other Oregon real estate agent, to represent you as a Seller's Agent, Buyer's Agent, or Disclosed Limited Agent, you should have a specific discussion with him/her about the nature and scope of the agency relationship. Whether you are a buyer or seller, you cannot make a licensee your agent without their knowledge and consent, and an agent cannot make you their client without your knowledge and consent.

Written Company Policy

863-015-0220 (1) Each real estate business shall develop and maintain a written company policy that sets forth the types of relationships real estate licensees associated with the business may establish. The policy shall include:

(a) Provisions on how licensees associated with the business will comply with the agency relationships set forth in OAR 863-015-0200;

(b) Procedures to ensure the protection of confidential information;

(c) Provisions regarding the supervision and control of licensees associated with the business in the fulfillment of their duties and obligations to their respective clients including but not limited to the requirements of OAR 863-015- 0205;

(d) Provisions regarding the supervision of licensed personal assistants employed by the brokerage or employed by licensees associated with the brokerage;

(2) The development and maintenance of a policy under this section shall not relieve a licensee from liability for the failure to maintain confidential information.

Oregon Unfair Trade Practices Act
(excerpts)

646.608 Unlawful business, trade practices; proof; Attorney General's rules. (1) A person engages in an unlawful practice when in the course of the person's business, vocation or occupation the person does any of the following:

(a) Passes off real estate, goods or services as those of another.

(b) Causes likelihood of confusion or of misunderstanding as to the source, sponsorship, approval, or certification of real estate, goods or services.

(c) Causes likelihood of confusion or of misunderstanding as to affiliation, connection, or association with, or certification by, another.

(d) Uses deceptive representations or designations of geographic origin in connection with real estate, goods or services.

(e) Represents that real estate, goods or services have sponsorship, approval, characteristics, ingredients, uses, benefits, quantities or qualities that they do not have or that a person has a sponsorship, approval, status, qualification, affiliation, or connection that the person does not have.

(f) Represents that real estate or goods are original or new if they are deteriorated, altered, reconditioned, reclaimed, used or secondhand.

(g) Represents that real estate, goods or services are of a particular standard, quality, or grade, or that real estate or goods are of a particular style or model, if they are of another.

(h) Disparages the real estate, goods, services, property or business of a customer or another by false or misleading representations of fact.

(i) Advertises real estate, goods or services with intent not to provide them as advertised, or with intent not to supply reasonably expectable public demand, unless the advertisement discloses a limitation of quantity.

(j) Makes false or misleading representations of fact concerning the reasons for, existence of, or amounts of price reductions.

(k) Makes false or misleading representations concerning credit availability or the nature of the transaction or obligation incurred.

(L) Makes false or misleading representations relating to commissions or other compensation to be paid in exchange for permitting real estate, goods or services to be used for model or demonstration purposes or in exchange for submitting names of potential customers.

(m) Performs service on or dismantles any goods or real estate when not authorized by the owner or apparent owner thereof.

(n) Solicits potential customers by telephone or door to door as a seller unless the person provides the information required under ORS 646.611.

(o) In a sale, rental or other disposition of real estate, goods or services, gives or offers to give a rebate or discount or otherwise pays or offers to pay value to the customer in consideration of the customer giving to the person the names of prospective purchasers, lessees, or borrowers, or otherwise aiding the person in making a sale, lease, or loan to another person, if earning the rebate, discount or other value is contingent upon occurrence of an event subsequent to the time the customer enters into the transaction.

(p) Makes any false or misleading statement about a prize, contest or promotion used to publicize a product, business or service.

(q) Promises to deliver real estate, goods or services within a certain period of time with intent not to deliver them as promised.

(r) Organizes or induces or attempts to induce membership in a pyramid club.

(s) Makes false or misleading representations of fact concerning the offering price of, or the person's cost for real estate, goods or services.

(t) Concurrent with tender or delivery of any real estate, goods or services fails to disclose any known material defect or material nonconformity.

(u) Engages in any other unfair or deceptive conduct in trade or commerce.

...

(2) A representation under subsection (1) of this section or ORS 646.607 may be any manifestation of any assertion by words or conduct, including, but not limited to, a failure to disclose a fact.

(3) In order to prevail in an action or suit under ORS 646.605 to 646.652, a prosecuting attorney need not prove competition between the parties or actual confusion or misunderstanding ....

Index

*Items in **bold** are main locations where the item is discussed in the text.*